ISBN: 979-8-8542-4034-5

Cover Image: *Prajñāpāramita.* She is the personification of the 'Perfection of Wisdom', '*prajñā*' meaning 'wisdom' and '*pāramita*' meaning 'perfection.

Painted by Ruth Perini (Srimukti) 2022.

Yoga Upanishad Series

1. *Yoga Chudamani Upanishad* by Swami Satyadharma 2003

2. *Yoga Tattwa Upanishad* by Swami Satyadharma
   translated by Ruth Perini 2015, 2018

3. *Yoga Darshana Upanishad* by Swami Satyadharma
   translated by Ruth Perini 2018

4. *Yoga Kundali Upanishad* by Swami Satyadharma
   translated by Ruth Perini 2019

5. *Nadabindu & Dhyanabindu Upanishads*
   by Swami Satyadharma, translated by Ruth Perini 2019

6. *Shandilya Upanishad* by Ruth Perini 2020

7. *Trishikhi Brahmanopanishad* by Ruth Perini 2021

Dedication

To all friends, practitioners and teachers of yoga, and to all seekers of spiritual wisdom, regardless of time or place, creed, gender, age or race.

Yoga Upanishad Series *Volume 8*

Yoga Upanishad Series *Volume 8*

Advaytaraka Upanishad
Mandalabrahmana Upanishad

Liberation Through Taraka Yoga

Original Sanskrit text with

Transliteration, Translation

and Commentary

by **Ruth Perini (Srimukti)**

CONTENTS

Introduction 1

Advaya-Tāraka-Upaniṣad

Invocation 10

Verses

1. Six Spiritual Qualities 11
2-4. Realising the Nature of Consciousness 12
5. Perception of the Inner Sign 15
6. Visions of Rays of Light 18
7-8. Tāraka, the Fivefold Space 21
9. Reflection of the Sun and Moon 25
10. Tāraka With and Without Form 27
11. Abode of Light 30
12. Śāmbhavī mudrā 32
13. Light, the Essence of the Inner Sign 34
14-18. The Spiritual Teacher 36
19. Liberation from Mundane Existence 39

Maṇḍala-Brāhmaṇa-Upaniṣad

Invocation 40

Verses

First Brāhmaṇa

First Section

1. Yājñavalkya approaches the Sun 42
2-3. Eightfold Path: The Yamas 44
4-5. The Niyamas 46
6-11. The Next Five Limbs 49

Second Section

1-3. The Five Defects 52
4-6. Tāraka 55
7-12. Effects of Tāraka 58
13-14. Final Effects of Tāraka 62

Third Section

1-6. Twofold Yoga: Tāraka and Amanaska 65

Fourth Section

1-4. Inner Object at Sahasrāra 71

Second Brāhmaṇa

First Section

1-4. Antarlakṣya: Cause of All 75
5. Experiences of Śāmbhavī 78
6-7. Three Views of Śāmbhavī 81
8-10. Signs of Śāmbhavī 83

Second Section
1-4. Praṇava 86
5. Rituals for Amanaska 91
Third Section
1-2. Freedom from Tripuṭī 94
3-4. Suṣupti and Samādhi 96
5-7. Becoming a Jīvanmukta 98
Fourth Section
1-3. Five States of Consciousness 101
4. Path to Liberation 104
5-6. Mind: Cause of Bondage and Liberation 108
Fifth Section
1-4. The Yogin as Brahman 110
Third Brāhmaṇa
First Section
1-2. Amanaska 113
3. Contemplating the Paramātmā 115
4-6. Undivided Bliss 118
Second Section
1-2. Becoming the Brahman 121
Fourth Brāhmaṇa
1-5. The Five Ethers 123
Fifth Brāhmaṇa
1-3. Dissolution of the Mind 126
4-5. Mind Dissolves in Viṣṇu 128
6-8. Perfection of the Non-dual State 130
9. The Avadhūta 132

APPENDICES
A End Notes 134
B References 138
C Pronunciation Guide 140
D Sanskrit Text 142
E Continuous Translation 161
F Swami Satyadharma 179
G Author's Note 183

Introduction

Veda is a Sanskrit word meaning 'knowledge'. In the context of the Vedas, it means 'revealed knowledge which is *śruti*, 'heard' from within, not taught. These ancient spiritual texts or hymns, through which we can learn much of the perceptions and insights of the early vedic seers, are grouped into four *samhitas* or collections: *Rig Veda, Yajur Veda, Sāma Veda* and *Atharva Veda*. They were revealed to enlightened beings 3,000 to 4,500 years ago or more (the Rig-Veda contains astronomical references describing occurrences in 5,000 to 3,000 BCE), and transmitted orally by the sages from generation to generation within brahmin families.

The four Vedas were considered to be divine revelations, and each word was carefully memorised. This was to ensure accurate transmission, but also because each syllable was considered to have spiritual power, its source being the supreme, eternal sound. This was a mammoth task, as there are 20,358 verses in the four Vedas, approximately two thousand printed pages. They were composed in fifteen different metres, which demanded perfect control of the breath. Georg Feuerstein describes them as 'a composite of symbol, metaphor, allegory, myth and story, as well as paradox and riddle' and their composers as 'recipients and revealers of the invisible order of the cosmos [with] inspired insights or illumined visions'.

Rig Veda

The Rig Veda is the oldest spiritual text in the world and still regarded as sacred, containing 1,028 hymns or songs of 10,589 verses in praise of the divine (*rig* or *ric* meaning 'praise'). Each hymn is recognised as a *mantra*, a sacred sound vibration, which releases energy from limited material awareness, thus expanding the consciousness. It is also the earliest surviving form of Sanskrit. The illumined seers composed the hymns while established in the highest consciousness, thus able to commune with luminous beings of the higher realms. There are about 250 hymns in praise of *Indra*, the divine force behind the ocean, heavens, thunder, lightning, rain and the light of the sun; 200 of *Agni*, born of the Sun, becoming the god of sacrificial fire, and over 100 of *Soma*, who gives immortality, and who is connected to the Sun, Moon, mountains, rivers and oceans. Others are dedicated to *Varuna*, who protects cosmic order; the *Ashvins*, supreme healers; *Ushas*, goddess of the dawn; *Aditi*, goddess of eternity; and *Saraswati*, goddess of the Vedas and of music and the arts.

Yajur Veda

The hymns of the Yajur-Veda, Veda of Sacrifice, consist of sacrificial formulas or prayers, including those of an internal or spiritual nature, which are chanted by the *adhvaryu* (priest), who performs the sacrifice. About a third of its 1,975 verses are taken from the Rig Veda. The rest are original and in prose form.

Sāma Veda

The Sāma Veda, Veda of Chants, gives instructions on the chanting of vedic hymns. The majority of its 1,875 verses are from the Rig Veda; only 75 verses are original. Many of the hymns were sung by special priests during sacrificial rites. Some are still sung today.

Atharva Veda

The Atharva Veda, named after the seer Atharvan, whose family were great seers in vedic times, contains 731 hymns of 5,977 verses, about one fifth of which are from the RigVeda. Much of the Atharva Veda consists of magical spells and charms for gaining health, love, peace and prosperity, or taking revenge on an enemy. Possibly for this reason, the Atharva Veda was either not accepted by the orthodox priesthood, or not given the same standing as the other Vedas.

The vedic people and their culture

The vedic people lived for over 2,500 years mainly along the banks of the Saraswati River, which was located in Northern India between the modern Ravi and Yamuna Rivers down to what is now the desert of Rajasthan. The Saraswati River dried up in about 1,900 BCE due to tectonic upheavals. Other areas of habitation included the Ganges River and its tributaries, rivers in Afghanistan (previously called Gandhara), the Himalayas and Mount Kailash in Tibet.

The vedic people had a complex multi-tiered view of the universe, in which humankind, nature and the divine are intertwined and interrelated. They had a deep knowledge of the oceans, mountains, deserts and forests of the physical world, as well as of the subtle worlds of deities and different levels of consciousness. People lived in cities or villages or were nomads, and were fully engaged in worldly life. They were an agrarian people, yet also had herds of cattle, horses and camels. Cities were constructed of stone, bricks and metal. They built chariots and ships. They were skilled workers in gold, metal, clay, stone, wood, leather and wool, and showed a very high standard in arts, crafts, astrology, medicine, music, dance and poetry.

After the Vedas

The Vedas were the foundation for the later revelations (*śruti*) in the *Brāhmaṇas* (ritual texts), the *Āranyakas* (texts on rituals and meditation for forest-dwelling ascetics) and the *Upaniṣads* (esoteric texts). Later still, the Vedas were the basis for numerous works of remembered or traditional knowledge, known as *smṛti,* including the epics: i.e. the *Mahābhārata, Rāmāyaṇa* and *Purāṇas,* and the *Sūtras,* or threads of knowledge, e.g. *Yoga Sūtras.* All these texts contain many concepts and practices, which come directly from the four Vedas.

Upaniṣads

The word *upaniṣad* is comprised of three roots: *upa* or 'near', *ni* or 'attentively', and *sad,* 'to sit'. The term describes the situation in which these unique texts were transmitted. The students or disciples sat near the realized master and listened attentively, as he expounded his experiences and understanding of the ultimate reality. These teachings are said to destroy the ignorance or illusion of the spiritual aspirant in regard to what is self and non-self, what is real and unreal, in relation to the absolute and relative reality. Only disciples were chosen, who had persevered in *sādhana catuṣṭaya*, the four kinds of spiritual effort, viz. *viveka* (discrimination between the permanent and impermanent), *vairagya* (non-attachment), *ṣadsampatti* (six virtues of serenity, self-control, withdrawal of the senses, endurance, perfect concentration and strong faith) and *mumukṣutva* (intense desire for liberation).

The Upaniṣads are derived from the Āranyakas, because they were chanted in the forest (*āranya*) after the aspirant had retired from worldly life. They are recorded in the later form of Sanskrit used in the Brāhmaṇas, and considered the last phase of *śruti*, vedic revelation. The Upaniṣads are regarded as *vedānta*, the end of the Vedas, inferring that *vedānta* is the end or completion of all perceivable knowledge, as they guide the aspirant beyond the limited mind to the *ātman* (spiritual self) and thus to *mokṣa* (liberation). Each upaniṣad reflected the teachings and tradition of a realized master, and was connected with a specific Veda and vedic school. It is estimated that there are over 200 Upaniṣads, which have been divided into seven groups: *Major*, *Vedānta*, *Śaiva, Śakta, Vaiśnava, Sannyasa* and *Yoga.*

Yoga Upaniṣads

The twenty-one Yoga Upaniṣads give an understanding of the hidden forces in nature and human beings, and describe esoteric yogic practices by which these forces can be manipulated and controlled. They emphasise that the inner journey to the one permanent reality, the *ātman*, is the essential one. Journeys to external places, such as holy sites and temples, as well as rituals and ceremonies, are not given importance. Their teachings give important information on the subtle body (*cakras, koṣas, prāṇa, kuṅḍalinī,* meditative states), and the tantric and yogic techniques, not given in the earlier upaniṣads, to attain them. Therefore, they are regarded as a significant integration of Vedanta and Tantra, which were previously considered incompatible. They are classified as 'minor' only because they postdate Adi Shankara.

Although their teachings actually predate Patañjali, the Yoga Upaniṣads were codified after the *Yoga Sūtras of Patañjali,* and form an important part of the classical yoga literature. However, they contain no references to Patañjali or his *Yoga Sūtras*. So, although the compilation of the Yoga Upaniṣads is post-Patañjali, the *vidyās*, or meditative disciplines, contained within them are pre-Patañjali. The Yoga Upaniṣads emerged at a time when the vedic and tantric cultures were coming together to share their knowledge. The wise thinkers from each culture sat down together and discussed how their insights and teachings could be combined in order to benefit humanity. Thus these upanisads combine the teachings of both tantra and yoga. It is evident in them that yoga leads to vedānta, and vedānta leads to yoga. However, they were written down by vedantic scholars and practitioners in order to show that these *vidyās* and related practices were not borrowed from Patañjali, but were known and practised from the ancient period.

Within the twenty-one Yoga Upaniṣads are six sub-groups which have their own main focus. The *Bindu Upaniṣads*, which include the *Amṛta-Bindu* (also known as the *Brahma-Bindu-Upaniṣad*), *Amṛta-Nada-Bindu*, *Nada-Bindu*, *Dhyāna-Bindu* and *Tejo-Bindu-Upaniṣads*, all concentrate on the bindu, the source or origin of all sound, and hence of creation. Bindu represents the transcendental sound manifested in the mantra *Aum*. The *Hamsa-Mantra*, *Soham*, is the main practice of the *Hamsa*, *Brahma-Vidya*, *Mahavakya* and *Paśupata-Brahma-Upaniṣads*. Concentration on *prāṇa*, the life force related to the process of inhalation and exhalation, brings the yogin to the knowledge of the transcendental self. The light of pure consciousness, which the enlightened irradiate, is the theme of the *Advaya-Taraka* and *Maṅḍala-Brahmana-Upaniṣads*. The *Kṣurika-Upaniṣad* (*kṣurika* meaning 'dagger') emphasises non-attachment as a means to liberation. The sixth group, comprised of eight late Yoga Upaniṣads from 1200 to 1300 A.D., covers teachings related to hatha and kundalini yogas. They are the *Yoga-Kuṅḍalī, Yoga-Tattwa, Yoga-Śikhā, Varāha, Śāndilya, Tri-Śikhi-Brahmana, Yoga-Darśana* and *Yoga-Chūdāmani Upaniṣads.*

Advaya-Tāraka and Maṇḍala-Brāhmaṇa Upaniṣads both describe the method of *Tāraka-Yoga*. They are connected to the *Shukla Yajurveda*.

Advaya-Tāraka-Upaniṣad is the upaniṣad of the non-dual (*advaya*) deliverer (*tāraka*). It is dated between 100 BCE and 300 CE. The word 'tāraka' means ferrying, carrying over or rescuing, star or raft. In this context it means 'ferrying one across the ocean of *saṃsāra*', liberation from the cycle of birth, death and rebirth, by dwelling in the radiant light of pure consciousness, which is the central theme of Vedānta philosophy, the identity of the Brahman with the innermost Self, the *ātman*. So Tāraka Yoga is the Self in the form of light.

The text begins by listing the six spiritual qualities necessary for progress on the spiritual path: equanimity, intense desire for liberation, endurance, sensory withdrawal and faith. The text begins by listing the six spiritual qualities necessary for progress on the spiritual path: equanimity, intense desire for liberation, endurance, sensory withdrawal and faith. It then describes the three *laksyas*, outer, intermediate and inner aims, each one giving insights, signs or visions. When the concentration is fixed on *bahirlakṣya*, the outer sign or aim, a variety of colours can be seen. *Madhyalakṣya*, the intermediate sign or aim, is the intermediate stage of *dhāraṇā*, concentration, where the mind has the experience of *pañcākāśa*, the five subtle luminous spaces of consciousness. Concentration on *antarlakṣya*, the inner sign, is concentration on the ascent of the *kundalini* up *brahma nāḍī* within *suṣumnā nāḍī* from *mūlādhāra cakra* to the crown of the head at *sahasrāra.* The yogin experiences sounds and visions coming from an internal source.

Tāraka is with form when experienced through the sense of sight, and without form when *ājñā cakra* is awakened and a radiant light, the essential form of the nondual Reality, is seen above it. This is achieved through the practice of *śāṃbhavī mudrā*, nosetip gazing, and hearing *praṇava*, the mantra AUM.

Finally the qualities of the true spiritual teacher are listed. This teacher is the one who can guide the yogin along the path to liberation, and whom the yogin experiences as a spiritual reality rather than a human personality.

Maṇḍala-Brāhmaṇa-Upaniṣad, a later, more extensive version of Advaya-Tāraka-Upaniṣad. Various scholars state its date of composition as early 1000 CE, after 10th century CE or the 14th century CE. Brāhmaṇa is the *puruṣa*, the Supreme Being, in the sphere of the Sun, who gives the Divine Knowledge to the great sage Yājñavalkya.

There are eighty-nine lengthy verses divided into five Brāhmaṇas, which are explanations of sacred knowledge and teachings. This work refers to the three visionary experiences (lakṣya) and the five types of 'ether-space' (*ākāśa*) known in tāraka-yoga. It further mentions three types of gaze (*dṛṣṭi*) during meditation. The goal is 'transmindedness' (*amanaskatā*), the condition of 'living liberation' (*jīvan-mukti*).'

Brāhmaṇa 1

The great sage Yājñavalkya requests Āditya, the Lord of the Sun, to describe the essence of the Soul. Āditya replies that the way to the essence of the Soul is the eightfold path of yoga. The eight steps are *yama, niyama, prāṇāyāma, pratyāhāra, dhāraṇā, dhyāna* and *samādhi.* The five obstacles on the path are sensual desire, anger, incorrect breathing, fear and sloth, which can be conquered by spiritual volition, patience and equanimity, a scant diet, concentration, truthfulness and integrity. Meditation on Tāraka, the light of yoga, is recommended, as Tāraka is the deliverer from the mundane existence of the cycle of conception, birth, life and death to *sat-cit-ānanda*: existence-consciousness-bliss, which are the three integral parts of Brahman, the ever-expanding consciousness, and leads to *amanaska*, when the mind is free from thought and desire.

Brāhmaṇa 2

The three *lakṣyas*, inner, intermediate and outer points on which one meditates, and their effects are described, as are the experiences of *śāmbhavī mudrā*, eyebrow centre gazing, leading to amanaska. *Praṇava* is the light of pure consciousness and the primal sound vibration of AUM. Certain rituals are described which lead to *dhyāna* and the light of *kaivalya*, final liberation in the state of consciousness, where all differences are unified. The difference between *suṣupti* (deep sleep) and *samādhi* is explained. The five states of consciousness are waking, dreaming, deep sleep, *turīya* (the fourth) and beyond *turīya.* The essential qualities of a true spiritual teacher are *viveka* (discrimination between the permanent and impermanent), *vairagya* (dispassion, letting go of desire for mundane enjoyments), *ṣaḍsampatti* (the six virtues of equanimity, self-control, sensory withdrawal, endurance, faith and constant concentration on reality) and *mumukṣutva* (intense desire for liberation). The mind is thus recognised as the cause of both bondage and liberation.

Brāhmaṇa 3
Amanaska is defined. Śāmbhavī mudrā leads to amanaska. By contemplating the *paramātman,* and living without all the senses, one attains the Supreme Reality.

Brāhmaṇa 4
Āditya describes the five kinds of ether: *ākāśa, parākāśa, mahākāśa, sūryākāśa* and *paramākāśa* and the importance of the nine *cakras*, six *ādhāras*, three *lakṣyas* [and] five *ākāśas.*

Brāhmaṇa 5
The thinking mind attached to sensual objects is in bondage, whereas the mind not attached to sensual objects becomes liberated. Attachment to sensual objects is enslavement of the mind. Through this dissolution of the mind, *nirvikalpa samādhi*, only pure consciousness remains. Finally the yogin becomes an *avadhūta*, free from all worldly attachments or mental illusions.

अद्वयतारकोपनिषद्

Advaya-Tārakopaniṣad

Opening Invocation

शान्तिपाठः

śāntipāṭhaḥ

ॐ पूर्णमिदः पूर्णमिदम् पूर्नापूर्णमुदच्यते ।

पूर्णस्य पूर्णमादाय पूर्णमेवावशिष्यते ।।

ॐ शान्तिः शान्तिः शान्तिः ।।

Om pūrṇamidaḥ pūrṇamidam pūrṇāpūrṇamudacyate
pūrṇasya pūrṇamādāya pūrṇamevāvaśiṣyate
om śāntiḥ śāntiḥ śāntiḥ

Vocabulary

Om: sound of creation; *pūrṇam-idaḥ*: that is full; *pūrṇam-idam*: this is full; *pūrṇā*: from the full; *pūrṇam-udacyate*: comes the full; *pūrṇam-ādāya*: if the full is taken; *pūrṇasya*: from the full; *pūrṇam-eva*: only the full; *avaśiṣyate*: remains; *om śāntiḥ*: peace of the divine.

Translation

Om, that is full, this is full. From the full comes the full. If the full is taken from the full, only the full remains.

Commentary

The spiritual aspirant invokes this *śānti* mantra before the commencement of the Upaniṣad. All the Upaniṣads begin with an invocation to a god or guru. Here the word 'full' means 'complete' or 'infinite', because only the infinite can be full, having neither beginning nor end. It refers to the unmanifest universe, which is full of divine consciousness, non-dual and unlimited.

Verse 1: Six Spiritual Qualities

अथातोऽद्वयतारकोपनिषदं व्याख्यास्यामो यतये
जितेन्द्रियाय शमदमादिंषड्गुणपूर्णाय ।।१।।

athāto'dvayatārakopaniṣadaṃ vyākhyāsyāmo yataye jitendriyāya śamadamādiṃṣaḍguṇapūrṇāya (1)

Vocabulary

athātaḥ: now; *syāma*: we have; *vyākhyā*: exposition; *yataye*: for the sage; *jitendriyāya*: for the ascetic; *pūrṇāya*: filled; *ṣaḍ-guṇa*: six qualities; *śama*: equanimity; *dama-ādim*: self-control etc.

Translation

Now we have an exposition of the *advaya-tāraka-upaniṣad* for the sage [and] ascetic [who is] filled [with] the six qualities of equanimity, self-control etc.

Commentary

According to the *aparokṣanubhūti*[1] (Direct Experience) by Ādi Śaṅkara, there are six qualities necessary for the serious spiritual aspirant. They are equanimity (*śama*), self-control (*dama*), sensory withdrawal (*uparati*), endurance (*titikṣa*), faith (*śraddha*) and constant meditation on the Supreme Reality (*samādhāna*).

Mind control is when the mind always rests on its aim. Self-control is control of the senses. Sensory withdrawal is withdrawal from or non-dependence of the mind on anything external; it is the ability to internalise. Endurance is endurance without complaint. Faith is the ability to understand the message of the scriptures and the guru's teachings. Constant meditation on the Supreme Reality is the perfect establishment of the higher mind (buddhi) in Brahman (the expanding reality), giving the ability to make right decisions.

Verses 2 to 4: Realising the Nature of Consciousness

चित्स्वरूपोऽहमिति सदा भावयन्त्सम्यङ् निमीलिताक्षः
किंचिदुन्मीलिताक्षो वान्तर्दृष्ट्या भ्रूदहरादुपरि
सच्चिद्नन्दतेजःकूटरूपं परम्ब्रह्मावलोकयंस्तद्रूपो भवति ।।२।।
गर्भजन्मजरामरणसंसारमहद्भयात्संतारयति तस्मात्तारकमिति ।
जीवेश्वरौ मायिकौ विज्ञाय सर्वविशेषं नेति नेतीति विहाय
यदवशिष्यते तदद्वयं ब्रह्म ।।३।।
तस्मिद्ध्यौ लक्ष्यत्रयानुम्संधानः कर्तव्यः ।।४।।

citsvarūpo'hamiti sadā bhāvayantsamyaṅ nimīlitākṣaḥ
kiṃcidunmīlitākṣo vāntardṛṣṭyā bhrūdaharādupari
saccidānandatejaḥkūṭarūpaṃ parambrahmāvalokayaṃ-
stadrūpo bhavati (2)
garbhajanmajarāmaraṇasaṃsāramahadbhayāt-
saṃtārayati tasmāttārakamiti
jīveśvarau māyikau vijñāya sarvaviśeṣaṃ neti
netīti vihāya yadavaśiṣyate tadadvayaṃ brahma (3)
tasmiddhyau lakṣyatrayānumsaṃdhānaḥ kartavyaḥ (4)

Vocabulary

sadā: always; *bhāvayant*: recognising; *aham*: I am; *svarūpa*: nature; *cit*: Consciousness; *samyak*: completely; *nimīlitākṣaḥ*: eyes shut; *va*: or; *kiṃcit*: somewhat; *unmīlitākṣaḥ*: eyes open; *antar-dṛṣṭyā*: by looking inward; *daharāt-upari*: slightly above; *bhrū*: eyebrows; *avalokayan*: beholding; *param-brahma*: Supreme Reality; *rūpam*: form; *kūṭa*: multitude; *tejaḥ*: fires; *sat-cit-ānanda*: Being-Consciousness-Bliss; *bhavati*: he becomes; *tat-rūpa*: that form.

tasmāt: thus; *saṃtārayati*: can save himself; *mahat-bhayāt*: from the great fear; *saṃsāra*: cycle; *garbha*: conception; *janma*: birth; *jarā*: old age; *maraṇa*: death; *tārakam-iti*: this is Tāraka; *vijñāya*: having discerned; *māyikau*: illusory; *jīva-īśvarau*: individual and transcendental; *vihāya*: having abandoned; *sarva-viśeṣam*: all differentiation; *iti*: saying; *neti neti*: not this, not that; *tad . . yad*: that which; *avaśiṣyate*: remains; *advayaṃ brahma*: non-dual Absolute.

tasmin dhyau: of that illumination; *anumsaṃdhānaḥ*: close attention; *kartavyaḥ*: should be made; *lakṣya-traya*: three signs.

Translation

Always recognising 'I am the nature of Consciousness', [with] eyes completely shut or eyes somewhat open, by looking inward slightly above the eyebrows, [then] beholding the Supreme Reality, [in] the form of a multitude [of] fires [of] Being-Consciousness-Bliss, one becomes that form.

Thus [the yogin] can save himself from the great fear of the cycle of conception, birth, old age [and] death. This is Tāraka. Having discerned the illusory individual and transcendental [and] abandoned all differentiation, saying 'not this, not that', that which remains is the nondual Absolute.

For the realisation] of that illumination, close attention should be made to the three signs.

Commentary

This is the central theme of Vedānta philosophy, the identity of the Brahman with the innermost Self, the ātman.

The *advaya-tāraka* (non-dual deliverer) is the transcendental consciousness which the yogin perceives through *ājñā cakra* as many lights. Ājñā cakra, also known as the third eye, is located at the top of the spinal column in the mid-brain, corresponding to the pineal gland. Concentrating on this area with the eyes shut or slightly open, the yogin perceives the light of pure consciousness. Having discriminated between the individual and the transcendental, he knows without doubt that he is one with pure consciousness, and no longer fears the worldly cycle of birth, death and rebirth.

The three *lakṣya* (signs, visions) are 'meditative visionary states marked by an intense experience of light'[2]. There are three variations: the external, internal and intermediate visions, described in the following verses.

Verse 5: Perception of the Inner Sign

देहमध्ये ब्रह्मनाडी सुषुम्ना सूर्यरूपिणी पूर्णचन्द्राभा वर्तते ।
सा तु मूलाधारादारभ्य ब्रह्मरन्ध्रगामिनी भवति ।
तन्मध्ये ताडित्कोटिसमानकान्त्या मृणालसूत्रवत्सूक्षमाङ्गी
सूक्ष्माङ्गी कुण्डलिनीति प्रसिद्धास्ति ।
तां दृष्ट्वा मनसैव नरः सर्वपापविनाशद्वारा मुक्तो भवाति ।
फालोर्ध्वगललाटविशेषमण्डले निरन्तरं
तेजस्तारकयोगविस्फुरणेन
पश्यति चेत्सिद्धे भवति ।
तर्जन्यग्रान्मीलितकर्णरन्ध्रद्वये तत्र फूत्कारशब्दो जायते ।
तत्र स्थिते मनसि चक्षुर्मध्यगतनीलज्योतिःस्थलं
विलोक्यान्तर्दृष्ट्या निरतिशयसुखं प्राप्नोति ।
एवं हृदये पश्यति ।
एवमन्तर्लक्ष्यणं मुमुक्षुभिरुपास्यम् ।।५।।

dehamadhye brahmanāḍī suṣumnā sūryarūpiṇī
pūrṇacandrābhā vartate
sā tu mūlādhārādārabhya brahmarandhragāminī bhavati
tanmadhye tāḍitkoṭisamānakāntyā mṛṇālasūtravatsūkṣmāṅgī
kuṇḍalinīti prasiddhāsti
tāṃ dṛṣṭvā manasaiva naraḥ sarvapāpavināśadvārā mukto
bhavati
phālordhvagalalāṭaviśeṣamaṇḍale nirantaraṃ
tejastārakayogavisphuraṇena paśyati cetsiddhe bhavati
tarjanyagrānmīlitakarṇarandhradvaye tatra phūtkāraśabdo
jāyate
tatra sthite manasi cakṣurmadhyagatanīlajyotiḥsthalaṃ
vilokyāntardṛṣṭyā niratiśayasukhaṃ prāpnoti
evaṃ hṛdaye paśyati
evamantarlakṣyaṇaṃ mumukṣubhirupāsyam (5)

Vocabulary

vartate: exists; *deha-madhye*: in the middle of the body; *sūrya-rūpiṇī*: of the form of the sun; *ābhā*: lustre; *pūrṇa-candra*: full moon; *ārabhya*: starting; *mūlādhārāt*: from the root *cakra*; *bhavati gāminī*: it extends to; *brahmarandhra*: *brahmarandhra*, the opening at the crown of the head; *tat-madhye*: in its centre; *asti*: is; *prasiddhā kuṇḍalinī*: renowned *kuṇḍalinī*; *kāntyā*: with a radiance; *samāna*: equal to; *koṭi*: crore, ten million; *tāḍit*: lightning flashes; *sūkṣmā-aṅgī*: subtle of limb; *vat*: like; *sūtra*: thread; *mṛṇāla*: fibrous lotus root; *tāṃ dṛṣṭvā*: having seen it; *manasā-eva*: through the mind alone; *naraḥ*: person; *bhavati*: becomes; *muktaḥ*: liberated; *vināśa-dvārā*: through the destruction; *sarva-pāpa*: all sin; *cet*: if; *nirantaram*: incessantly; *paśyati*: he sees; *visphuraṇena*: with eyes wide open; *tejaḥ*: radiance; *phāla-ūrdhva-ga*: leaping forth; *viśeṣa-maṇḍale*: in a specific area; *lalāṭa*: forehead; *siddhe bhavati*: he is an adept; *tatra*: then; *phūtkāra-śabdaḥ*: blowing sound; *dvaye karṇa-randhra*: in the two ear orifices; *mīlita*: blocked; *agrāt*: with the tips; *tarjani*: forefingers; *vilokya*: beholding; *sthite manasi*: in [that] firm state of mind; *sthalam*: place; *nīla-jyotiḥ*: blue light; *gata*: gone to; *cakṣuḥ-madhya*: middle of the eyes; *prāpnoti*: he attains; *antar-dṛṣṭyā*: by looking inwards; *niratiśaya-sukham*: unequalled bliss; *paśyati evam*: he realises thus; *hṛdaye*: in the heart; *evam upāsyam*: such [is] the perception; *antaḥ-lakṣyaṇam*: inner sign; *mumukṣubhiḥ*: by those wishing for liberation.

Translation

[There] exists in the middle of the body the *brahmanāḍī* [within] *suṣumnā*, of the form of the sun [and] the lustre of the full moon. Arising from the root *cakra*, it extends to the *brahmarandhra*, the opening at the crown of the head. In its centre is the renowned *kuṇḍalinī*, with a radiance equal to a crore of lightning flashes [and] subtle [of] limb like the thread [of] the fibrous lotus root. Having seen it through the mind alone, a person becomes liberated through the destruction of all sin. If he incessantly sees with eyes wide open the radiance of *tāraka-yoga* leaping forth in a specific area from the forehead, he is an adept. Then the blowing sound *phū* is produced in the two ear orifices, blocked with the tips of the forefingers. Then, beholding in [that] firm state of mind [that] place [as] a blue light gone to the middle of the eyes, he attains, by looking inward, unequalled bliss. He realises thus in the heart. Such [is] the perception [of] the inner sign by those wishing for liberation.

Commentary

Concentration on *antar lakṣya*, the inner sign, begins with the awareness or vision of the *suṣumnā nāḍī* which contains in its centre another *nāḍī* called the *brahma nāḍī*. It is through the brahma nāḍī that the *kuṇḍalinī* travels from the base of the spine at *mūlādhāra cakra* to the crown of the head at *sahasrāra*. Visualisation of brahma nāḍī as the form of a luminous thread as bright as thousands of flashes of lightning leads to the liberation from the bondage of past actions. If the yogin continues to see this luminous thread at ājñā cakra with open eyes, he is perfected in yoga. Other signs that the kuṇḍalinī has reached ājñā cakra is a subtle sound such as blowing or hissing coming from an internal source and a blue light at both ājñā cakra, the eyebrow centre, and *anāhata cakra*, the heart centre. Now when he looks inward he has the experience of the ultimate bliss in both mind and heart.

'This is the completion of antar lakṣya *dhāraṇā*, which is subtle, psychic concentration, holding the mind to an inner experience and having darśan of it, not just imagining it.'[3]

Verse 6: Visions of Rays of Light

अथ बहिर्लक्ष्यणं नासिकाग्रे चतुर्भिः
षद्भिरष्टभिर्दशभिर्द्वादशभिः क्रमादङ्गुलान्ते
नीलद्युतिश्यामत्वसदृग्रक्तभङ्गीस्फुरत्पीतशुक्लवर्ण-
द्वयोपेतव्योम यदि पश्यति स तु योगी भवति ।
चलदृष्ट्या व्योम भागवीक्षितुः पुरुषस्य दृष्ट्यग्रे
ज्योतिर्मयूखा वर्तन्ते ।
तद्दर्शनेन योगी भवति ।
तप्तकाञ्चनसंकाशज्योतिर्मयूखा अपाङ्गान्ते
भुमौ वा पश्यति तद्दृष्टिः स्थिरा भवति ।
शीर्षोपरि द्वादशाङ्गुलसमीक्षितुरमृतत्वं भवति ।
तत्र कुत्र स्थितस्य शिरसि व्योमज्योतिर्दृष्टं
चेत्स तु योगी भवाति ।।६।।

atha bahirlakṣyaṇaṃ nāsikāgre caturbhiḥ
sadbhiraṣṭabhirdaśabhirdvadaśabhiḥ kramādaṅgulānte
nīladyutiśyāmatvasadṛgraktabhaṅgīsphuratpītaśuklavarṇa-
dvayopetavyoma yadi paśyati sa tu yogī bhavati
caladṛṣṭyā vyoma bhāgavīkṣituḥ puruṣasya
dṛṣṭyagre jyotirmayūkhā vartante
taddarśanena yogī bhavati
taptakāñcanasaṃkāśajyotirmayūkhā apāṅgānte
bhumau vā paśyati taddṛṣṭiḥ sthirā bhavati
śīrṣopari dvādaśāṅgulasamīkṣituramṛtatvaṃ bhavati
tatra kutra sthitasya śirasi vyomajyotirdṛṣṭaṃ
cetsa tu yogī bhavati (6)

Vocabulary

atha: now; *bahiḥ-lakṣyaṇam*: external sign; *yadi*: if; *paśyati*: he sees; *nāsikāgre*: nosetip; *caturbhiḥ-sadbhiḥ-aṣṭabhiḥ-daśabhiḥ-dvadaśabhiḥ*: four, six, eight, ten, twelve;

aṅgulānte: digit lengths; *kramāt*: respectively; *vyoma*: space; *dvaya-upeta*: doubly endowed with; *śukla*: bright; *pīta*: yellow; *varṇa*: colour; *sphurat*: quivering; *bhaṅgī*: wave; *rakta*: red; *sadṛk*: like; *dyuti*: glistening; *nīla*: blue; *śyāmatva*: dark blue; *tu*: then; *sa bhavati yogī*: he is a yogin; *vartante*: there are; *jyotiḥ-mayūkhāḥ*: rays of light; *dṛṣṭi-agre*: foremost range of vision; *puruṣasya*: of the person; *bhāga-vīkṣituḥ*: scanning; *cala-dṛṣṭyā*: with wandering vision; *vyoma*: space; *tat-darśanena*: by seeing that; *yogī bhavati*: he becomes a yogin.

Translation

Now the external sign [is described]. If he sees [at a distance from] the nosetip of four, six, eight, ten [and] twelve digit-lengths respectively a space doubly endowed with a bright yellow colour, a quivering wave [of] red-like glistening [and] dark blue, then he is a yogin. There are rays of light in the foremost range of vision of the person scanning with wandering vision the space. By seeing that, he becomes a yogin.

[When] he sees rays of light sparkling like molten gold at the outer corners of the eyes or on the ground, that vision is fixed. [Whoever] sees twelve digit-lengths above the head attains immortality. If [he has] the vision [of] the lustre of space in the head, wherever he is, is indeed a yogin.

Commentary

This verse describes the colours that can be seen in *bahirlakṣya*, the outer sign or aim, which the yogin focuses on to enter the state of deep concentration. Different colours will be seen depending on their distance from the nosetip. They are respectively bright yellow, reddish and dark blue. When the vision is perfectly steady, rays of golden light can be seen at the outer corners of the eyes or on the ground. Concentration on bahirlakṣya awakens *iḍā* and *piṅgalā nāḍīs* which are on the left and right side of suṣumnā nāḍī. Blue represents iḍā, and gold, piṅgalā. When the vision expands to twelve digit-lengths above the head, the light of *sahasrāra cakra* at the crown of the head is seen, the yogin transcends the limited individual self.

Verses 7 and 8: Tāraka, the Fivefold Space

अथ मध्यलक्ष्यणं प्रातश्चित्रादिवर्णाखण्डसूर्यचक्रवद्वह्नि-
ज्वालावलीवत्तद्विहीनान्तरिक्षवत्पश्यति ।
तदाकाराकारितयावतिष्ठति ।
तद्भूयोदर्शनेन गुणरहिताकाशं भवति ।
विस्फुरत्तारकारसंदीप्यमानागाढतमोपमं परमाकाशं भवति ।
कालानलसमद्योतमानं महाकाशं भवति ।
सर्वोत्कृष्टपरमद्युतिप्रद्योतमानं तत्त्वाकाशं भवति ।
कोटिसूर्यप्रकाशवैभवसंकाशं सूर्याकाशं भवति ।
एवं बाह्याभ्यन्तरस्थव्योमपञ्चकं तारकलक्ष्यम् ।
तद्दर्शी विमुक्तफलस्ताद्दव्योमसमानो भवति ।
तस्मात्तारक एव लक्ष्यममनस्कफलप्रदं भवति ॥७॥
तत्तारकं द्विधं पूर्वार्धतारकमुत्तरार्धममनस्कं चेति ।
तदेष श्लोको भवति ।
तद्योगं च द्विधा विद्धि पूर्वोत्तरविधानतः ।
पूर्वं तु तारकं विद्यादमनस्कं तदुत्तरमिति ॥८॥

atha madhyalakṣyaṇaṃ prātaścitrādivarṇākhaṇḍa-
sūryacakravadvahnijvālāvalīvattadvihīnāntarikṣavat paśyati
tadākārākāritayāvatiṣṭhati
tadbhūyodarśanena guṇarahitākāśaṃ bhavati
visphurattārakākārasaṃdīpyamānāgāḍhatamopamaṃ
paramākāśaṃ bhavati
kālānalasamadyotamānaṃ mahākāśaṃ bhavati
sarvotkṛṣṭaparamadyutipradyotamānaṃ
tattvākāśaṃ bhavati
koṭisūryaprakāśavaibhavasaṃkāśaṃ sūryākāśaṃ bhavati
evaṃ bāhyābhyantarasthavyomapañcakaṃ tārakalakṣyam
taddarśī vimuktaphalastādṛgvyomasamāno bhavati
tasmāttāraka eva lakṣyamamanaskaphalapradaṃ bhavati (7)

tattārakaṃ dvividhaṃ pūrvārdhatārakamuttarārdham-
amanaskaṃ ceti
tadeṣa śloko bhavati
tadyogaṃ ca dvidhā viddhi pūrvottaravidhānataḥ
pūrvaṃ tu tārakaṃ vidyādamanaskaṃ taduttaramiti (8)

Vocabulary

atha: now; *madhya-lakṣyaṇam*: intermediate sign; *paśyati*: sees; *varṇa*: coloured; *citra-ādi*: various images; *prātaḥ*: in the early morning; *akhaṇḍa*: whole; *sūrya-cakra-vat*: like the orb of the sun; *āvalī-vat*: like a row; *jvāla*: flames; *vahni*: fire; *antarikṣa-vat*: like the regions between heaven and earth; *tat-vihīna*: without these; *ākāritaya*: having the shape of; *tat-ākāra*: this form; *avatiṣṭhati*: he abides; *tat darśanena*: by seeing this; *bhūyaḥ*: again; *bhavati*: he becomes; *ākāśa*: space; *guṇarahita*: devoid of qualities; *bhavati paramākāśam*: he becomes the supreme space; *upamam*: resembling; *āgāḍha-tamaḥ*: unfathomable darkness; *saṃdīpyamāna*: radiant with; *visphurat*: dazzling; *ākāra*: form; *bhavati mahākāśam*: he becomes the great space; *bhavati tattvākāśam*: he becomes the elemental space; *pradyotamānam*: radiant with; *parama-dyuti*: supreme lustre; *utkṛṣṭa*: superior; *sarva*: all; *bhavati sūryākāśam*: he becomes the solar space; *saṃkāśam*: appearance; *prakāśa-vaibhava*: dazzling glory; *koṭi-sūrya*: hundred thousand suns; *evam*: thus; *pañcakam vyoma*: fivefold space; *bāhyābhyantara*: external and internal; *stha*: is; *tāraka-lakṣyam*: sign of *tāraka*, the deliverer; *darśī*: [whoever] experiences; *tat*: this; *vimukta-phalaḥ*: freed from the fruit; *bhavati*: becomes; *samānaḥ*: like; *tādṛg-vyoma*: such space; *tasmāt*: thus; *eva*: only; *lakṣyam*: sign; *tāraka*: *tāraka*, deliverer; *bhavati pradam*: is the bestower; *phala*: fruit; *amanaska*: *amanaska*, mindlessness.

tat-tārakam: that tāraka; *dvividham*: twofold; *pūrva*: earlier; *ardha*: half; *ca-iti*: and is; *uttara-ardham*: latter half; *amanaskam*: mindlessness; *bhavati*: there is; *ślokaḥ*: verse;

tadeṣa: about this; *iti*: saying; *tat-yogam*: that yoga; *dvidhā viddhi*: twofold way; *vidhānataḥ*: made of; *pūrva-uttara*: earlier and latter; *pūrvam vidyāt*: earlier is known as; *tu*: and; *tat-uttaram*: the latter; *amanaskam*: mindlessness.

Translation

Now the intermediate sign [is described]. [The yogin] sees various coloured images in the early morning like the whole orb of the sun [or] like a row of flames of fire [or] like the regions between heaven and earth without these. Having the shape of this form, he abides there. By seeing this again [and again] he becomes the space devoid of qualities. He becomes the supreme space resembling the unfathomable darkness radiant with the dazzling form of tāraka. He becomes the great space like the illumination of the fire of time. He becomes the elemental space, radiant with supreme lustre, superior [to] all. He becomes the solar space, [having the] appearance [of] the dazzling glory of a hundred thousand suns. Thus the fivefold space, external and internal is the sign of tāraka, the deliverer. [Whoever] experiences this, freed from the fruit, becomes like such space. Thus only the sign of tāraka is the bestower [of] the fruit [of] amanaska, mindlessness.

That tāraka [is] twofold: the earlier half is tāraka and the latter half mindlessness. There is a verse about this saying: 'That yoga [is] the twofold way, made of the earlier and the latter. The earlier is known as tāraka, and the latter mindlessness'.

Commentary

The verse describes the intermediate sign or aim, *madhya-lakṣya*. This is the intermediate stage of *dhāraṇā*, concentration where the mind has the experience of space. Concentrating here, the yogin sees colours resembling the whole sun or a never-ending row of blazing fire, or even just the space between heaven and earth. He becomes this form and abides there in the *vyoma pañcaka* or *pañcākāśa*, the five subtle luminous spaces of consciousness: *guṇa-rahita-ākāśa*, the space without qualities; *paramākāśa*, the supreme space, the state of *śūnya*, emptiness; *mahākāśa*, the great space, as bright as the centre of the sun; *tattvākāśa*, the elemental space, is the essence from which the elements originate; and *sūryākāśa*, the solar space, the pure luminous space of the sun or the soul. Having merged with them, freed from the fruits of his actions, he is delivered by tāraka to *amanaska*, the state free from thought.

Verse 9: Reflection of the Sun and Moon

अक्ष्यन्तस्तारयोश्चन्द्रसूर्यप्रतिफलनं भवाति ।
तारकाभ्यां सूर्यचन्द्रमण्डलदर्शनं ब्रह्माण्डमिव
पिण्डाण्ड्शिरोमध्यस्थाकाशे रवीन्दुमण्डलद्वितयमस्तीति
निश्चित्य तारकाभ्यां तद्दर्शनमात्राण्युभयैक्यदृष्ट्या-
मनोयुक्तं ध्यायेत् ।
तद्योगाभावे इन्द्रियप्रवृत्तेरनवकाशात् ।
तस्मादन्तर्दृष्ट्या तारक एवानुसंधेयः ।।९।।

akṣyantastārayoścandrasūryapratiphalanaṃ bhavati
tārakābhyāṃ sūryacandramaṇḍaladarśanaṃ
brahmāṇḍamiva
piṇḍāṇḍśiromadhyasthākāśe ravīndumaṇḍaladvitayamastīti
niścitya tārakābhyāṃ taddarśanamātrāṇyubhayaikyadṛṣṭyā-
manoyuktaṃ dhyāyet
tadyogābhāve indriyapravṛtteranavakāśāt
tasmādantardṛṣṭyā tāraka evānusaṃdheyaḥ (9)

Vocabulary

tārayoḥ: in the pupils; *akṣyantaḥ*: in the interior of the eyes; *bhavati*: there is; *pratiphalanam*: reflection; *candra-sūrya*: sun and moon; *darśanam*: seeing; *sūrya-candra-maṇḍala*: sun and moon discs; *tārakābhyām*: through the pupils; *iva*: like; *brahmāṇḍam*: macrocosm; *piṇḍāṇḍ*: microcosm; *ākāśe*: in the space; *śiraḥ-madhya*: centre of the head; *niścitya*: having ascertained; *asti*: it is; *dvitayam*: double; *ravīndu-maṇḍala*: point on the disc; *dhyāyet*: one should contemplate; *manaḥ-yuktam*: with fixed mind; *dṛṣṭyā*: through the perception; *ṇyubhaya*: looking upon the two; *ekya*: as one; *tat-darśana*: looking there; *mātrā*: for some time; *tārakābhyām*: through the pupils; *tat-yoga-abhāve*: without this connection; *anavakāśāt*: no scope; *indriya-pravṛtteḥ*: for the way of the senses; *tasmāt*: thus; *tāraka anusaṃdheyaḥ*:

tāraka should be investigated; *antardṛṣṭyā*: through introspection; *eva*: only.

Translation

In the pupils in the interior of the eyes, there is the reflection of the sun and moon. Seeing the sun and moon discs through the pupils is like [seeing] the macrocosm as the microcosm in the space in the centre of the head, having ascertained it is the double point on the disc. One should contemplate with fixed mind, through the perception [of] looking upon the two as one, looking there for some time through the pupils, [as] without this connection, [there is] no scope for the way of the senses. Thus tāraka should be investigated through introspection only.

Commentary

The verse propounds the concept that the macrocosm and microcosm are mirror images of each other. If the yogin sees reflection of the sun and moon in the pupils of the eyes, he can conclude that, as in the macrocosm, there exists a corresponding pair of the sun and moon discs in the ether in the middle of the head. If he sees the two as essentially one, he has transcended the duality and play of the senses. Thus it is only through introspection that tāraka, the deliverer, can be realised.

Verses 10: Tāraka with and without Form

तत्तारकं द्विविधं मूर्तितारकममूर्तितारकं चेति ।
यदिन्द्रियान्तं तन्मूर्तिमत् ।
यद्भ्रूयुगातीतं तदमूर्तिमत् ।
सर्वत्रान्तःपदार्थविवेचने मनोयुक्ताभ्यास इष्यते तारकाभ्यां
सदूर्ध्वस्थ सत्त्वदर्शनान्मनोयुक्तेनान्तरीक्षणेन
सच्चिद्नन्दस्वरूपं ब्रह्मैव ।
तस्माच्छुक्लतेजोमयं ब्रह्मेति सिद्धम् ।
तद्ब्रह्म मनःसहकारिचक्षुषान्तर्दृष्ट्या वेद्यं भवति ।
वममूर्तितारकमपि मनोयुक्तेन चक्षुषैव दहरादिकं वेद्यं
भवति रूपग्रहणप्रयोजनस्य मनश्चक्षुरधीनत्वाद्बाह्यवदान्तरे-
ऽप्यात्ममनश्चक्षुःसंयोगेनैव रूपग्रहणकारयोदयात् ।
तस्मान्मनोयुक्तान्तर्दृष्टिस्तारकप्रकाशा भवति ।।१०।।

tattārakaṃ dvividhaṃ mūrtitārakamamūrtitārakaṃ ceti
yadindriyāntaṃ tanmūrtimat
yadbhrūyugātītaṃ tadamūrtimat
sarvatrāntaḥpadārthavivecane
manoyuktābhyāsa iṣyate tārakābhyāṃ
sadūrdhvastha sattvadarśanānmanoyuktenāntarikṣaṇena
saccidānandasvarūpaṃ brahmaiva
tasmācchuklatejomayaṃ brahmeti siddham
tadbrahma manaḥsahakāricakṣuṣāntardṛṣṭyā vedyaṃ bhavati
evamamūrtitārakamapi manoyuktena cakṣuṣaiva daharādikaṃ
vedyaṃ bhavati rūpagrahaṇaprayojanasya
manaścakṣuradhīnatvādbāhyavadāntare'pyātmamanaś-
cakṣuḥsaṃyogenaiva rūpagrahaṇakāryodayāt
tasmānmanoyuktāntardṛṣṭistārakaprakāśā bhavati (10)

Vocabulary

tat-tārakam: that tāraka; *iti*: is; *murti-tārakam*: tāraka with form; *ca*: and; *amūrti-tārakam*: tāraka without form; *yat*: that which; *indriya-antam*: stops with the senses; *tat-mūrtimat*: that [is] with form; *bhrū-yuga-atītam*: transcends the pair of eyebrows; *tat-amūrtimat*: that [is] without form; *sarvatra*: in every case; *abhyāsa*: constant practice; *manaḥ-yuktam*: of a fixed mind; *iṣyate*: is necessary; *tārakābhyām*: through the pupils; *sattva-darśanāt*: pure vision; *sad-ūrdhvastha*: that which dwells beyond; *antarikṣaṇena*: through introspection; *manaḥ-yuktena*: through a steady mind; *sat-cit-ānanda*: Being-Consciousness-Bliss; *iva*: as; *svarūpam*: essential nature; *tasmāt*: hence; *mayam*: consisting of; *śukla-tejaḥ*: white radiance; *iti siddham*: is clear; *tat-brahma*: that Brahman; *bhavati vedyam*: becomes known; *antardṛṣṭyā*: through introspection; *cakṣuṣa*: by the eye; *manaḥ-sahakāri*: assisted by the mind; *evam api*: thus also; *amūrti-tārakam*: formless tāraka; *manaḥ-yuktena*: through the fixed mind; *cakṣuṣa-eva*: through the eye alone; *dahara-ādikam*: minuscule and others; *bhavati vedyam*: become known; *adhīnatvāt*: because of the dependence; *manaḥ-cakṣuḥ*: mind and eye; *prayojanasya*: for the purpose of; *rūpa-grahaṇa*: perception of form; *bāhyavat-āntare*: external and internal; *saṃyogena-eva*: only through the combination; *ātma-manaḥ-cakṣuḥ*: eye, mind and Self; *kārya*: action; *rūpa-grahaṇa*: perception of form; *udayāt*: can succeed; *tasmāt*: thus; *antardṛṣṭiḥ*: inner vision; *manaḥ-yukta*: fixed mind; *bhavati*: becomes; *tāraka-prakāśā*: light of tāraka.

Translation

That tāraka is twofold: tāraka with form and tāraka without form. That which stops with the senses [is] with form. That which transcends the pair of eyebrows [is] without form. In every case in examining the inner object, constant practice with a fixed mind is necessary. Through the pupils [and] the pure vision [of] that which dwells beyond, through introspection and a steady mind, [the yogin experiences] Being-Consciousness-Bliss as the essential nature [of]

Brahman. Hence Brahman, consisting of white radiance, is clear. That Brahman becomes known by the eye, assisted by the mind in introspection. Thus also the formless tāraka [is known]. Through the fixed mind, through the eye alone, the minuscule and others become known. Because of the dependence of mind and eye for the purpose of perception of form, external and internal, [it is] only through the combination of the eye, mind and Self [that] the action of perception of form can succeed. Thus inner vision [with] a fixed mind becomes the light of tāraka.

Commentary

The yogin can experience tāraka through the sense of sight as a defined shape, or without form as space or ether when it transcends the pair of eyebrows, awakening ājñā cakra, and expanding intuition and inner awareness. In both cases constant meditation practice is necessary to visualise the supreme reality as existence- consciousness-bliss in its innate form. Then the dazzling white lustre of the supreme reality, Brahman, becomes clear.

The heart centre is called in yoga *hṛdayākāśa*, 'the space within the heart where purity resides'[4]. It is traditionally symbolised by a lotus with twelve petals, in the centre of which 'burns the *akhaṇḍa jyotir*, the unflickering eternal flame, representing the *jīvātma* or individual soul'.[5] 'The minuscule space at the heart, has from ancient times been considered a locus of the effulgent transcendental Self'.[6] The others refer to the spaces of *cidākāśa*, the inner space visualised in meditation at ājñā cakra, and *dahārākāśa*, the deep space encompassing the lower cakras.

As perception is dependent on both the mind and the eye, both outwardly and inwardly, therefore the combination of mind, eye and Self is essential for the manifestation of Tāraka.

Verse 11: Abode of Light

भ्रूयुगमध्यबिले दृष्टिं तद्द्वारोर्ध्वस्थिततेज आविर्भूतं
तारकयोगो भवति ।
तेन सह मनोयुक्तं तारकं सुसंयोज्य प्रयत्नेन भ्रूयुग्मं
सावध्नानतया किंचिदूत्क्षेपयेत् ।
इति पूर्वभागी तारकयोगः ।
उत्तरं त्वमूर्तिमदमनस्कमित्युच्यते ।
तालुमूलोर्ध्यभागे महान् ज्योरिर्मयूखो वर्तते ।
तद्योगिभिर्ध्येयम् ।
तस्मादणिमादिसिसिद्धिर्भवति ॥११॥

bhrūyugamadhyabile dṛṣṭiṃ taddvārordhvasthitateja
āvirbhūtataṃ tārakayogo bhavati
tena saha manoyuktaṃ tārakaṃ susaṃyojya prayatnena
bhrūyugmaṃ sāvadhānatayā kiṃcidūtkṣepayet
iti pūrvabhāgī tārakayogaḥ
uttaraṃ tvamūrtimadamanaskamityucyate
tālumūlordhvabhāge mahān jyotirmayūkho vartate
tadyogibhirdhyeyam
tasmādaṇimādisiddhirbhavati (11)

Vocabulary

dvārā: by means of; *dṛṣṭim*: sight; *bile*: on the cavern; *bhrūyuga-madhya*: centre of the pair of eyebrows; *tejaḥ*: radiance; *sthita*: dwelling; *ūrdhva*: above; *bhavati*: becomes; *āvirbhūtatam*: visible; *tena*: through this; *susaṃyojya*: having united; *sāvadhānatayā prayatnena*: with careful effort; *tārakam manaḥ-yuktam*: tāraka [and] the fixed mind; *ūtkṣepayet*: should raise; *bhrūyugmam*: pair of eyebrows; *kiṃcit*: somewhat; *iti pūrva-bhāgī*: this is the former part; *uttaram*: latter; *tu*: however; *iti amūrtimat*: is without form; *ucyate*: is said; *amanaskam*: beyond the mind; *vartate*: there exists; *mahān*: great; *jyotirmayūkhaḥ*: ray of light; *bhāge*: in the part; *ūrdhva*: above; *tālu-mūla*: root of the palate; *tat dhyeyam*: it should be meditated on; *yogibhiḥ*: by the yogins; *tasmāt*: from that; *bhavati*: comes; *siddhiḥ*: power; *aṇima-ādi*: aṇima and others.

Translation

By means of the sight [being fixed] on the cavern [in] the centre of the pair of eyebrows, the radiance dwelling above becomes visible. [This is] tāraka yoga. Through this, having united with careful effort tāraka [and] the fixed mind, [the yogin] should raise the pair of eyebrows somewhat. This is the former part of tāraka yoga. The latter, however, is without form [and] is said [to be] beyond the mind. There exists a great ray of light in the part above the root of the palate. It should be meditated on by the yogins. From that comes the power [of] aṇima and others.

Commentary

The verse describes the way through the former tāraka which is with form to the latter tāraka without form. The yogin should meditate with fixed attention on ājñā cakra, the space behind the eyebrow centre. Eventually he will see the radiant light above it. This is the former part of tāraka yoga. The latter part of tāraka yoga is without form, and has transcended the mind. A great beam of radiance exists above the root of the palate. The aspiring yogin should meditate on this. As a result supernatural powers will flow.

The eight *siddhis*, supernatural powers, acquired by yogins who have practised intense meditation for a long time, are described in the commentary on verse 4 of *Maṇḍala-brāhmaṇa Upaniṣad*. They result from the opening of the cakras, which gives power over the elements. They can be an obstacle on the path of self-realisation, as they maintain an attachment to the illusory world.

Verse 12: Śāṃbhavī Mudrā

अन्तर्बाह्यलक्ष्ये दृष्टौ निमेषोन्मेषवर्जितायां सत्यां
शांभवी मुद्रा भवति ।
तन्मुद्रारूढज्ञानिनिवसद्भूमिः पवित्रा भवति ।
तद्दृष्ट्वा सर्वे लोकाः पवित्रा भवन्ति ।
तादृशपरमयोगिपूजा यस्य लभ्यते सो'पि मुक्तो भवति
॥१२॥

antarbāhyalakṣye dṛṣṭau nimeṣonmeṣavarjitāyāṃ satyāṃ
śāṃbhavī mudrā bhavati
tanmudrārūḍhajñāninivāsādbhūmiḥ pavitrā bhavati
taddṛṣṭvā sarve lokāḥ pavitrā bhavanti
tādṛśaparamayogipūjā yasya labhyate so'pi mukto bhavati
(12)

Vocabulary
dṛṣṭau: if there is the vision; *antarbāhya-lakṣye*: inner and outer sign; *varjitāyām*: devoid of; *nimeṣa-unmeṣa*: opening and closing the eyes; *bhavati*: this is; *satyāṃ śāṃbhavī mudrā*: true *śāṃbhavī mudrā*; *nivāsāt*: because of the sojourn; *jñāni*: sages; *rūḍha*: ascended to; *tat-mudrā*: this mudrā; *bhūmiḥ bhavati*: earth becomes; *pavitrā*: purified; *tat-dṛṣṭvā*: having seen this; *sarve lokāḥ*: all worlds; *bhavanti pavitrā*: are purified; *saḥ yasya*: he who; *labiate*: is permitted; *pūjā*: homage to; *tādṛśa-parama-yogi*: such great yogins; *bhavati api*: is also; *muktaḥ*: liberated.

Translation
If there is the vision of the inner and outer sign, [at the same time] devoid [of the power] of opening and closing the eyes, this is the true śāṃbhavī mudrā. Because of the sojourn of sages [who have] ascended to this mudrā, the earth becomes purified. Having seen this, all worlds are purified. He who is permitted homage to such great yogins is also liberated.

Commentary

Śāṃbhavī mudrā is a meditative practice where the gaze is fixed internally at the eyebrow centre. The practice begins with the eyes open, gazing upward at the eyebrow centre without blinking for as long as possible, while inwardly contemplating the transcendental Self. Eventually a light may appear in *cidākāśa*, the space in the mind in the region of ājñā cakra. Then, when the eyes are closed, the yogin should concentrate on the central point of that light. If he can see the light of both the inner and outer sign at the same time without opening or closing the eyes, then he is in *śāṃbhavī mudrā*.

'Śāṃbhavī is the wife or consort of Śambhu and both are aspects of Śakti and Lord Śiva [Śambhu meaning 'benign' or 'benevolent']. According to tradition, Śambhu taught Śāṃbhavī the practice of *śāṃbhavī mudrā* as a means of attaining higher awareness. It is said that practising this mudra will stir Śambhu and make him appear, meaning that it will induce higher consciousness within the practitioner.' [7]

Verse 13: Light, the Essence of the Inner Sign

अन्तर्लक्ष्यजलज्योतिःस्वरूपं भवति ।

परमगुरूपदेशेन सहस्रारे जलज्योतिर्वा बुददहिगुहानिहितज्योतिर्वा

षोडशान्तस्थतुरीयचैतन्यं वान्तर्लक्ष्यं भवति ।

तद्दर्शनं सदाचार्यमूलम् ।।१३।।

antarlakṣyajalajyotiḥsvarūpaṃ bhavati
paramagurūpadeśena sahasrāre jalajyotirvā
buddhiguhānihitajyotirvā ṣoḍaśāntasthaturīyacaitanyaṃ
vāntarlakṣyaṃ bhavati
taddarśanaṃ sadācāryamūlam (13)

Vocabulary

jala-jyotiḥ: radiant light; *antarlakṣya*: inner sign; *bhavati*: is; *svarūpam*: its essential form; *upadeśena*: through instruction; *parama-guru*: superior spiritual teacher; *sahasrāre*: at the thousand-petalled; *vā*: or; *jyotiḥ*: light; *nihita*: concealed in; *buddhi-guhā*: cavern of the buddhi; *vā turīya-caitanyam*: or the fourth consciousness; *stha*: abiding; *ṣoḍaśa-anta*: at the end of the sixteenth; *tat-darśanam*: sight of that; *mūlam*: dependent on; *sat-ācārya*: true teacher.

Translation

The radiant light [of] the inner sign is the essential form of the nondual Reality. Through instruction by a superior spiritual teacher, the inner sign becomes the radiant light at the thousand-petalled [lotus] or the light hidden in the cavern of the *buddhi*, or the fourth consciousness abiding at the end of the sixteenth. The sight of that [is] dependent on a true teacher.

Commentary

The light radiated through internal meditation is of one's own form. Through the guidance of a teacher who has attained the highest states of meditation, the vision is of the transcendental light at *sahasrāra cakra*, the thousand-petalled lotus at the crown of the head, or the light in the buddhi, the higher mind and seat of wisdom, or the fourth consciousness which links and transcends the waking, dream and sleeping states and which is situated sixteen digits above the crown of the head. It is only through the grace of this teacher that the yogin has this vision.

Verses 14 to 18: The Spiritual Teacher

आचार्या वेदसम्पन्नो विष्णुभक्तो विमत्सरः ।
योगज्ञो योगनिष्ठश्च सदा योगात्मकः शुचिः ॥१४॥
गुरुभक्तिसमायुक्तः पुरुषज्ञो विशेषतः ।
एवं लक्षणसंपन्नो गुरुरित्यभिधीयते ॥१५॥
गुशब्दस्त्वन्धकातः स्याद्रुशब्दस्तन्निरोधकः ।
अन्धकारनिरोधित्वाद्रगुरुरित्यभिधीयते ॥१६॥
गुरुरेव परं ब्रह्म गुरुरेव परा गतिः ।
गुरुरेव परा विद्या गुरुरेव परायणम् ॥१७॥
गुरुरेव परा काष्ठा गुरुरेव परं धनम् ।
यस्मात्तदुपदेष्टासौ तस्माद्गुरुतरो गुरुरिति ॥१८॥

ācāryā vedasampanno viṣṇubhakto vimatsaraḥ
yogajño yoganiṣṭhaśca sadā yogātmakaḥ śuciḥ (14)
gurubhaktisamāyuktaḥ puruṣajño viśeṣataḥ
evaṃ lakṣaṇasaṃpanno gururityabhidhīyate (15)
guśabdastvandhakāraḥ syādruśabdastannirodhakaḥ
andhakāranirodhitvādgururityabhidhīyate (16)
gurureva paraṃ brahma gurureva parā gatiḥ
gurureva parā vidyā gurureva parāyaṇam (17)
gurureva parā kāṣṭhā gurureva paraṃ dhanam
yasmāttadupadeṣṭāsau tasmādgurutaro gururiti (18)

Vocabulary

ācāryāḥ: spiritual teacher; *veda-sampannaḥ*: conversant in the *vedas*; *viṣṇu-bhaktaḥ*: devotee of Viṣṇu; *vimatsaraḥ*: free from jealousy; *yoga-niṣṭhaḥ*: intent on yoga; *yoga-jñaḥ*: wisdom of yoga; *ca sadā*: and always; *śuciḥ*: pure; *yoga-ātmakaḥ*: pure nature of yoga; *samāyuktaḥ*: endowed with; *guru-bhakti*: devotion to the teacher; *viśeṣataḥ*: especially; *puruṣa-jñaḥ*: knower of the Self; *evam*: thus; *sampannaḥ*: possessed with; *lakṣaṇa*: qualities; *abhidhīyate*: is deemed;

guru: spiritual teacher; *tu*: now; *gu-śabdaḥ*: sound *gu*; *syāt*: is; *andhakāraḥ*: darkness; *ru-śabdaḥ*: sound *ru*; *tat-nirodhakaḥ*: its obstruction; *nirodhitvāt*: because of the obstruction; *guruḥ abhidhīyate*: he is named a *guru*; *guruḥ-eva*: guru alone; *param brahma*: supreme reality; *parā gatiḥ*: supreme way; *parā vidyā*: supreme knowledge; *parāyaṇam*: supreme refuge; *yasmāt*: because; *asau tat-upadeṣṭaḥ*: the teacher of That; *tasmāt*: therefore; *guruḥ-iti*: guru is; *gurutaraḥ*: greater.

Translation

A spiritual teacher [is] conversant in the *vedas*, a devotee of Viṣṇu, free from jealousy, intent on yoga, [has] the wisdom of yoga, and always [in] the pure nature of yoga. [He who is] endowed with devotion to the teacher [and who is] especially a knower of the Self, thus possessed with [these] qualities is deemed a spiritual teacher. Now the sound *gu* is darkness. The sound *ru* is its obstruction. Because of the obstruction of darkness, he is named a *guru*. The guru alone [is] the Supreme Reality. The guru alone [is] the supreme way. The guru alone [is] supreme knowledge. The guru alone [is] the supreme refuge. The guru alone [is] the supreme aim. The guru alone [is] supreme wealth. Because he [is] the teacher of that, therefore the guru is greater.

Commentary

These verses list the qualities of the true guru. He has the sacred knowledge revealed in the Vedas to sages and seers over seven thousand years ago. He is a devotee of Viṣṇu, the Supreme Consciousness, preserver of the universe. He is pure, devoid of jealousy, anger and other negative qualities. Here the word 'yoga' which is derived from the verbal root '*yuj*', to yoke or join', means uniting with the pure consciousness, Brahman. Thus the guru, by dispelling the darkness of ignorance, reveals the radiant light of Brahman.

In the Bhagavad Gita, Chapter 2, Vs 55 to 57, Arjuna asks Krishna how to recognise a teacher who has reached the highest states of meditation. Krishna answers that 'one who, having renounced all desires born of the mind, is satisfied in the Self and by the Self, is said to be one whose insight is steady. In the midst of suffering and happiness, his mind is neither confused nor kindled. He who is freed from desires, passion, fear and anger, is said to be a sage of tranquil mind. One who is free from all material desires, who is neither delighted nor disturbed by joys and sorrows is the one who stands firm in wisdom.[8]

Verse 19: Liberation from Mundane Existence

यः सकृदुच्चारयति तस्य संसारमोक्षनं भवति ।
सर्वजन्मकृतं पापं तत्क्षणादेव नश्यति ।
सर्वान्कामानवाप्नोति ।
सर्वपुरुषार्थसिद्धिर्भवति ।
य एवं वेदेत्युपनिषत् ॥१९॥

yaḥ sakṛduccārayati tasya saṃsāramokṣanaṃ bhavati
sarvajanmakṛtaṃ pāpaṃ tatkṣaṇādeva naśyati
sarvānkāmānavāpnoti
sarvapuruṣārthasiddhirbhavati
ya evaṃ vedetyupaniṣat (19)

Vocabulary
yaḥ: whoever; *uccārayati*: causes to be uttered; *sakṛt*: once; *bhavati*: becomes; *saṃsāramokṣanam*: liberated from mundane existence; *tat-kṣaṇāt-eva*: at that very moment; *pāpam kṛtam*: sin committed; *sarva-janma*: every birth; *naśyati*: disappears; *avāpnoti*: he gains; *sarvāt-kāmāt*: all desires; *bhavati*: he has; *siddhiḥ*: fulfilment; *sarva-puruṣa-artha*: all human goals; *yaḥ*: whoever; *veda evam*: knows this; *upaniṣat*: upaniṣad.

Translation
Whoever causes [this] to be uttered once becomes liberated from mundane existence. At that very moment the sin committed [in] every birth disappears. He gains all desires. He has fulfilment of all human goals. Whoever knows this [knows] the upaniṣad.

॥ इति अद्वयतारकोपनिषत्समाप्ता ॥

iti advayatārakopaniṣat-samāptā
Thus concludes the Advaya-Tāraka-Upaniṣad.

मण्डलब्राह्मण उपनिषद्
Maṇḍalabrāhmaṇa Upaniṣad

Opening Invocation

।।शान्तिपाठः।।
śāntipāṭhaḥ

ब्राह्मान्तस्तरकारं व्योमपञ्चकविग्र।
राजयोगैकसंसिद्धं रामचन्द्रमुपास्महे।।१।।
ॐ पूर्णमदः इति शान्तिः।
brāhmāntastārakākāraṃ vyomapañcakavigraham
rājayogaikasaṃsiddhaṃ rāmacandramupāsmahe (1)
Om pūrṇamadaḥ iti śāntiḥ

Vocabulary
upāsma-he: remember; *rāmacandram*: Rāmacandra; *eka-saṃsiddham*: the one accomplished; *vigraham*: expansion; *pañcaka*: five; *vyoma*: subtle spaces; *tāraka-ākāram*: form of *tāraka*; *brāhma-antaḥ*: within Brāhman; *Om*: sound of creation; *pūrṇam-adaḥ*: that is full; *om iti śāntiḥ*: om is divine peace.

Translation
Remember Rāmacandra, the one accomplished [in] *rāja yoga*, the expansion of the five subtle spaces, the form of *tāraka* within Brāhman.
That [is] full. Om is divine peace.

Commentary
The spiritual aspirant invokes this *śānti mantra* before the commencement of the Upaniṣad.

Rāmacandra or Rāma was the ruler of the ancient kingdom of

Kosala and the hero of the *Rāmāyana*. In the *Vaiṣṇava* tradition he is worshipped as an incarnation of Viṣṇu. He has reached the highest states of meditation (*rāja yoga*), merging with Brahman as the form of luminous consciousness in the five etheric dimensions.

All the Upaniṣads begin with an invocation to a god or guru. Here the word 'full' means 'complete' or 'infinite', because only the infinite can be full, having neither beginning nor end. It refers to the unmanifest universe, which is full of divine consciousness, non-dual and unlimited.

||प्रथमं ब्राह्मणम्||
prathamaṃ brāhmaṇan

First Brāhmaṇa

||प्रथमः खण्डः||
prathamaḥ khaṇḍaḥ

First Section

Verse 1: Yājñavalkya approaches the Sun

याज्ञवल्क्यो ह वै महामुनिरादित्यलोकं जगाम ।
तमादित्यं नत्वा भो भगवन्नादित्यात्मतत्त्वमनुब्रूहीति ||१||
yājñavalkyo ha vai mahāmunirādityalokaṃ jagāma
tamādityaṃ natvā bho
bhagavannādityātmatattvamanubrūhīti (1)

Vocabulary
mahā-muniḥ yājñavalkyaḥ: great sage Yājñavalkya; *jagāma*: went to; *āditya-lokam*: world of the Sun; *natvā*: bowing to; *ādityam*: Sun; *iti tam*: he said to Him; *bho bhagavan-āditya*: o blessed Lord Āditya; *anubrūhi*: describe; *ātma-tattvam*: essence of the soul.

Translation
The great sage Yājñavalkya went to the world of the Sun. Bowing to the Sun, he said to Him: 'o blessed Lord Āditya, describe [to me] the essence of the soul'.

Commentary
Yājñavalkya is the name of several teachers over different eras. One is the yogin of the *bṛhadāranyaka-upaniṣad*, whose teachings included the concepts of rebirth (*punar-janman*)

and *karma*. The *Yājñavalkya-Smṛti*, the subject of which is *dharma* (law and ethics), was written in the third century BCE. by a later Yājñavalkya. It maintains that dharma is the highest ideal, leading to *ātma-darśan*, vision of the Higher Self. The *Yoga-Yājñavalkya-Samhitā* may have been written by this Yājñavalkya, or by the later master yogin who is the disciple in this upaniṣad and others.

Āditya refers to the sun as a deity. The Sun is the soul, makes its own fire and light, and is therefore creator of all. The Vedic Astrology (*jyotiṣa*) considers the Sun to be the soul, moving from lifetime to lifetime. Thus it is the Sun to whom the brahmin poses the fundamental questions of existence, while, perhaps, he gazes at its solar magnificence as it appears on the horizon.

Verses 2 and 3: Eightfold Path: The Yamas

स होवाच नारायणः ।

ज्ञानयुक्तयमाद्यष्टाङ्गयोग उच्यते ॥२॥

शीतोष्णाहारनिद्राविजयः सर्वदा शान्तिर्निश्चलत्वं

विषयेन्द्रियनिग्रहश्चैते यमाः ॥३॥

sa hovāca nārāyaṇaḥ
jñānayuktayamādyaṣṭāṅgayoga ucyate (2)
śītoṣṇāhāranidrāvijayaḥ sarvadā śāntirniścalatvaṃ
viṣayendriyanigrahaścaite
yamāḥ (3)

Vocabulary

sa nārāyaṇaḥ: he, Nārāyaṇa; *ha uvāca*: replied thus; *ucyate*: it is said; *aṣṭāṅga-yoga*: eightfold [path of] yoga; *yama-ādi*: beginning with *yama*; *jñāna-yukta*: combined with *jñāna*; *vijayaḥ*: conquest; *śītoṣṇa*: cold and heat; *āhāra-nidrā*: food and sleep; *sarvadā*: constant; *niścalatvam*: unchangeable; *śāntiḥ*: peace; *ca*: and; *nigrahaḥ*: restraint; *viṣaya-indriya*: sense organs; *ete yamāḥ*: these [are] the yamas.

Translation

He, Nārāyaṇa, replied thus: it is said [to be] the eightfold [path of] yoga beginning with *yama* [and] combined with *jñāna*. The conquest of cold and heat, food and sleep, constant unchangeable peace and the restraint [of] the sense organs, these [are] the yamas.

Commentary

Āditya begins to describe the path to the essence of the soul. This path is known as the eightfold path of yoga which leads to spiritual wisdom. The eight limbs are described in verses 2 to 11. The first limb is *yama*, rules of behaviour with others and moral self-restraints and forbearance, which strengthen and calm the mind. In this text there are four yamas, *viz* mastery at all times over heat and cold as well as food and sleep; peace which cannot be disturbed (*śānti*); steadiness (*niścalatva*) of the mind; restraint of the senses from external objects.

Other yoga systems and classical texts list different yamas. For example, the *Rāja Yoga Sūtras* of Patañjali, describe five yamas: *ahimsā*, non-violence, *satya*, truthfulness in speech, *asteya*, honesty in action, *brahmacarya*, abstinence or moderation in sexual conduct, and *aparigraha*, non-possessiveness.

Nārāyaṇa (*lit.* descendant of man) is another name for Sūrya (sun) and Viṣṇu, as they are the supporters of life.

Verses 4 and 5: The Niyamas

गुरुभक्तिः सत्यमर्गानुरक्तिः सुखागतवस्तवनुभवश्च
तद्वस्त्वनुभवेन ।
तुष्टिर्निःसङ्गत्ता एकान्तवासो मनोनिवृत्तिः फलानभिलाषो
वैराग्यभावश्च नियमाः ।।४।।
सुखासनवृत्तिश्चिरवासश्चैवमासननियमो भवति ।।५।।

gurubhaktiḥ satyamārgānuraktiḥ
sukhāgatavastvanubhavaśca tadvastvanubhavena
tuṣṭirniḥsaṅgattā ekāntavāso manonivṛttiḥ phalānabhilāṣo
vairāgyabhāvaśca niyamāḥ (4)
sukhāsanavṛttiściravāsaścaivamāsananiyamo bhavati (5)

Vocabulary

niyamāḥ: *niyamas*; *guru-bhaktiḥ*: devotion to *guru*; *anuraktiḥ*: dedication to; *satya-mārga*: path of truth; *vastu-anubhavaḥ*: enjoyment of things; *sukha-āgata*: come from joy; *ca tad-vastu-anubhavena*: and through the enjoyment of these things; *tuṣṭiḥ*: contentment; *niḥsaṅgattā*: detachment; *ekānta-vāsaḥ*: secluded abode; *manaḥ-nivṛttiḥ*: cessation of thought; *ca vairagya-bhāvaḥ*: and an attitude of detachment; *phalān-abhilāṣaḥ*: craving for the fruits; *āsana sukha-āsana*: āsana [which is] a comfortable posture; *vṛttiḥ-ciravāsaḥ*: mind for a long time; *bhavati evam niyamaḥ*: is indeed a niyama.

Translation

The *niyamas* [are] devotion to *guru*, dedication to the path of truth, enjoyment of things [which] come from joy, and through the enjoyment of these things, contentment, detachment, a secluded abode, cessation of thought and an attitude of detachment [from] the craving for the fruits [of actions]. An āsana [which is] a comfortable posture [with] a [steady] mind for a long time is indeed a niyama.

Commentary
Self-restraint (*niyama*), the second limb, consists of practices of personal discipline leading to self-purification. They are internal disciplines, which allow the practitioner to gain control over the senses and manage the mind at a deeper level.

The first niyama is **devotion to *guru***, who has realised the Self, and in this liberated state can dispel the darkness of the disciple's ignorance. The disciple forms a spiritual link to the teacher, rather than a psychological connection.

Adherence to the path of truth: the *Yoga Darśana Upaniṣad* says 'that which is seen, heard and smelt through the sense organs of the eyes etc is said to be *satyam,* as *Brahman* is no different from that. The highest truth is that *Brahman* is everywhere and not elsewhere'.[2] The ultimate truth is that Brahman, the universal consciousness, is all-pervading; it is the substratum of existence, which pervades everything everywhere. The experience and understanding of the nature of Brahman leads to the highest truth, satyam.

Enjoyment of things which come from joy, knowing that they all come from Brahman. One can enjoy whatever is experienced through the five senses, remembering that they arise in the material world from Brahman.

'Becoming indifferent to obtaining one's desire, and free from attachment everywhere, until one has realised Brahman, is known as the supreme ***santoṣa***.[3] Santoṣa means that inner contentment or satisfaction, which is not influenced by craving or obtaining external things. ***Niḥsaṅgatā*** meaning non-attachment, that is, indifference to worldly desires, including spiritual ambitions, such as fame and the acquisition of powers which are distractions from the meditative state.

Living in solitude in a **secluded abode**: the yogin who is dedicated to progress in yoga should have a secluded place in which to practise, free from noise, pollution and distractions of all kinds. Here the mind can become tranquil and free from thought.

Cessation of thought can be achieved by dedicated practice of the yamas and niyamas.

Detachment from the craving for the fruits of one's actions is the yoga of dynamic meditation or *karma yoga*, the yoga of action, as explained in the third chapter of the *Bhagavad Gītā* (vs 17-19), thus transcending the individual self. Karma yoga means 'action done without selfish desire, purely as duty or sacrifice, does not bind but liberates'.[4]

Postural restraint (***āsana-niyama***) is a comfortable seated posture that can be maintained over a long period of time for the purpose of meditation.

Other versions of the niyamas are described in the *Yoga Sūtra* of Patañjali and the *Yoga Darśana Upaniṣad.* Patañjali's *Yoga Sūtra* lists five niyamas: *śauca* (cleanliness, purity), *santoṣa* (contentment), *tapas* (austerity), *svādhyāya* (self-study) and *īśvara-praṇidhāna* (devotion to the Lord).[5]
The ten niyamas in *Yoga Darśana Upaniṣad* are *tapas*, austerity, endurance; *santoṣa*, contentment; *āstika*, faith in the highest consciousness; *dāna*, charity, giving to others; *iśvara pūja*, worship of the highest consciousness; *siddhanta śravana*, listening to the scriptures; *hrīḥ,* remorse or shame; *mati*, desire for humility; *japa*, repetition of *mantra,* syllables or words of power; and *vrata*, vow or commitment.[6]

Verses 6 to 11: The Next Five Limbs

पूरककुम्भकरेचकैः षोडशचतुःषष्टिद्वात्रिंशत्संख्यया यथाक्रमं प्राणायामः ।।६।।

विषयेभ्य इन्द्रियार्थेभ्यो मनोनिरोधनं प्रत्याहारः ।।७।।

विषयव्यावर्तनपूर्वकं चैतन्ये चेतःस्थापनं धारणं भवति ।।८।।

सर्वशरीरेषु चैतन्यैकतानता ध्यानम् ।।९।।

धयाहविस्मृतिःसमाधिः ।।१०।।

एवं सूक्ष्माङ्गानि ।

य एवं वेद स मुक्तिभाग्भवति ।।११।।

pūrakakumbhakarecakaiḥ
ṣoḍaśacatuḥṣaṣṭidvātriṃśatsaṃkhyayā
yathākramaṃ prāṇāyāmaḥ (6)
viṣayebhya indriyārthebhyo manonirodhanaṃ pratyāhāraḥ (7)
viṣayavyāvartanapūrvakaṃ caitanye cetaḥsthāpanam dhāraṇaṃ bhavati (8)
sarvaśarīreṣu caitanyaikatānatā dhyānam (9)
dhyānavismṛtiḥsamādhiḥ (10)
evaṃ sūkṣmāṅgāni
ya evaṃ veda sa muktibhāgbhavati (11)

Vocabulary

pūraka-kumbhaka-recakaiḥ: through inhalation, breath retention and exhalation; *saṃkhyayā*: with the count of; *ṣoḍaśa*: sixteen; *catuḥṣaṣṭi*: sixty-four; *dvātriṃśat*: thirty-two; *yathākramam*: respectively; *manaḥ-nirodhanam*: restraining of the mind; *viṣayebhyaḥ indriyārthebhyaḥ*: from the objects of the senses; *dhāraṇaṃ bhavati*: *dhāraṇa* is; *viṣaya-vyāvartana-pūrvakam*: drawing away from objects; *cetaḥ*: mind; *sthāpanam*: fixing; *caitanye*: on consciousness; *caitanya-ekatānatā*: attention fixed on the one consciousness;

sarva-śarīreṣu: in all bodies; *evam sūkṣma-aṅgāni*: these are the subtle limbs; *ya veda evam*: whoever knows this; *sa mukti-bhāgbhavati*: he attains liberation.

Translation

Prāṇāyāma [is] through inhalation, breath retention and exhalation, with the count of sixteen, sixty-four and thirty-two [*mātrās*] respectively. *Pratyāhāra* [is] the restraining of the mind from the objects of the senses. *Dhāraṇa* is drawing the mind away from objects [of the senses and] fixing [it] on consciousness. *Dhyāna* [is] the attention fixed on the one consciousness in all bodies. *Samādhi* is the forgetting [of the individual self] in *dhyāna*. These are the subtle limbs [of yoga]. Whoever knows this, he attains liberation.

Commentary

The practice of *prāṇāyāma* uses the breath to control the flowof *prāṇa* within the body, *prāṇa* meaning life-force or vitalenergy, *āyāma* meaning expansion. It has three phases: inhalation, retention and exhalation. The yoga upaniṣads recommend that prāṇāyāma be performed in the ration of 16:64:32. The basic ratio of 1:1:1 should be practised and gradually increased withut straining.

A *mātrā* is a unit of measurement. It is defined in *Yoga Cud-mani Upaniṣad* as the time a single breath takes to fill the lungs. According to *Yoga Tattwa Upaniṣad* it is the time taken to snap one's fingers after circling the knee with the hand. The *Tattwa Vaiṣāradī* says one must circle the kneethree times. The *Mārkandeva Purāṇa* says it is the time taken to open and close one's eyes.

Pratyāhāra is the first limb of the inner path of meditation. In the path of *aṣṭāṅga yoga*, the eightfold yoga, the first four limbs are known as *bahiraṅga*, or outer branches. The last four are called *antaraṅga*, the inner branches. Pratyāhāra is the fifth limb of aṣṭāṅga yoga and the first limb on the inner path, which leads to the following levels of *dhāraṇā*, one-pointed concentration, *dhyāna*, spontaneous meditation, and finally *samādhi*, transcendental consciousness.

Once one has control of all the vital energies through *prāṇāyāma*, one understands that everything comes from *mahāprāṇa*, the cosmic unmanifest *prāṇa.* When the mind is first introverted, it withdraws and disassociates from the five senses of sound, touch, sight, taste and smell. This process is called *pratyāhāra*. Having withdrawn the senses, one is able to concentrate on a symbol of higher consciousness, given by the guru or of one's own choice. This is called *dhāraṇā*. Then keeping the mind on the thought '*so'ham*', '*so*' representing cosmic consciousness, and '*ham*' individual consciousness, leads spontaneously to deep meditation, *dhyāna*. When there is no thought in the mind, only pure awareness, this is the state of *samādhi.*[7]

Once the yogin is established in the practices of yama, niyama, āsana and prāṇāyāma and pratyāhāra, then *dhāraṇā*, full concentration, comes naturally, leading to the attainment of pure consciousness.

'Whoever knows this' means whoever has fully internalised and assimilated the practices.

||द्वितीयः खण्डः||
dvitīyaḥ khaṇḍaḥ
Second Section

Verses 1 to 3: The Five Defects

देहस्य पञ्च दोषा भवन्ति कामक्रोधनिःश्वासभयनिद्राः ||१||
तन्निरासस्तु निःसंकल्पक्षमालघ्वाहाराप्रमादतातत्त्वसेवनम्
||२||
निद्राभयसरीसृपं हिंसादितरङ्गं तृष्णावर्तं दारपङ्कं संसारवार्धिं
तरीतुं सूक्ष्ममार्गवलम्ब्य सत्त्वादिगुणानतिक्रम्य
तारकमवलोकयेत् ||३||
dehasya pañca doṣā bhavanti
kāmakrodhaniḥśvāsabhayanidrāḥ (1)
tannirāsastu
niḥsaṃkalpakṣamālaghvāhārāpramādatātattvasevanam (2)
nidrābhayasarīsṛpaṃ hiṃsāditaraṅgaṃ tṛṣṇāvartaṃ
dārapaṅkaṃ
saṃsāravārdhiṃ tarītuṃ sūkṣmamārgavalambya
sattvādiguṇānatikramya tārakamavalokayet (3)

Vocabulary *bhavanti*: there are; *pañca doṣāḥ*: five faults; *dehasya*: in the body; *kāma*: sensual desire; *krodha*: anger; *niḥśvāsa*: incorrect breathing; *bhaya*: fear; *nidrā*: sleep; *tat-nirāsaḥ*: removal of these; *tattva-sevanam*: reverence for the *tattvas*; *pramādatā*: caution; *laghu-āhāra*: light diet; *kṣamā*: forbearance; *niḥsaṃkalpa*: lack of desires; *tarītum*: to cross; *saṃsāra-vārdhim*: ocean of *saṃsāra*; *sarīsṛpam*: serpent; *nidrā-bhaya*: sleep and fear; *taraṅgam*: wave; *hiṃsā-ādi*: violence etc; *āvartam*: whirlpool; *tṛṣṇā*: greed; *paṅkam*: mire; *dāra*: wife; *ālambya*: adhering to; *sūkṣma-mārgau*: subtle paths; *anatikramya*: without transgressing; *guṇa*: quality; *sattva-ādi*: *sattva* etc; *tārakam-avalokayet*: one should observe *Tāraka.*

Translation

There are five faults in the body: sensual desire, anger, incorrect breathing, fear [and] sleep. The removal of these [can be achieved by] reverence for the *tattvas*, caution, a light diet, forbearance [and] lack of desires. To cross the ocean of *saṃsāra* [which is] the serpent of sleep and fear, the wave of violence etc, the whirlpool of greed, the mire of a wife, adhering to the subtle paths [and] without transgressing the quality of *sattva* etc, one should observe *Tāraka*.

Commentary

The five faults in the body are inherent defects, imperfections or hindrances which prevent us from reaching the highest state of perfection. They are conquered by spiritual volition (*samkalpa*), patience and equanimity (*kṣamā),* a scant diet (*laghu-āhāra*), concentration, truthfulness and integrity.

When breathing is incorrect, prāṇa is not retained and toxins are not exhaled. To correct the breathing one should perform *nāḍī śodhana prāṇāyāma*, the breath balancing practice, starting with 1:1:1as the basic ratio of inhalation, breath retention and exhalation. This ratio can be gradually increased. An advanced practitioner who has mastered the initial stages of the practice may increase the ratio to 16:64:32. The practice of kumbhaka, internal breath retention, conserves the prāṇa in order to awaken consciousness by activating *suṣumnā*, the spiritual flow of energy. In order for meditation to be successful, it is necessary to first balance the breath, which controls the mental and vital energies, and then activate suṣumnā, the spiritual force.[8]

Saṃsāra is worldly existence which is the endless cycle of birth, death and rebirth, where the *tamasic* forces represented by crawling serpents, constant violence, the turbulence of greed and the swamp of sensual pleasure. Without moving away from harmony and purity, one should keep to the meditative path, concentrating on the light of *Tāraka* who ferries one across the ocean of saṃsāra.

Verses 4 to 6: Tāraka

भ्रूमध्ये सच्चिदानन्दतेजःकूटरूपं तारकं ब्रह्म ।।४।।

तदुपायं लक्ष्यत्रयावलोकनम् ।।५।।

मूलाधारादारब्य ब्रह्मरन्ध्रपर्यन्तं सुषुम्ना सूर्यभा ।

तन्मध्ये ताडत्कोटिसमा मृणालतन्तुसूक्ष्मा कुण्दलिनी ।

तत्र तमोनिवृत्तिः ।

तद्दर्शनात्सर्वपापनिवृत्तिः ।।६।।

bhrūmadhye saccidānandatejaḥkūṭarūpaṃ tārakaṃ brahma (4)
tadupāyaṃ lakṣyatrayāvalokanam (5)
mūlādhārādārabya brahmarandhraparyantaṃ suṣumnā sūryabhā
tanmadhye tāḍatkoṭisamā mṛṇālatantusūkṣmā kuṇḍalinī
tatra tamonivṛttiḥ
taddarśanātsarvapāpanivṛttiḥ (6)

Vocabulary
tāraka: deliverer; *rūpam*: form; *kūṭa*: unchanging; *tejaḥ*: spirit; *sat-cit-ānanda*: existence-consciousness-bliss; *brahma*: Brahman; *bhrūmadhye*: at the eyebrow centre; *avalokanam*: seeing; *lakṣya-traya*: through the three points of concentration; *tat-upāyam*: way to it; *ārabya*: from; *paryantam*: up to; *sūryabhā*: bright as the sun; *tanmadhye*: in its centre; *samā*: as; *tāḍat-koṭi*: crores of lightning; *sūkṣmā*: subtle; *mṛṇālatantu*: fibrous root of a lotus; *tamaḥ-nivṛttiḥ*: destruction of *tamas*; *tatra*: there; *tat-darśanāt*: through insight into it; *sarva-pāpa-nivṛttiḥ*: destruction of all sins.

Translation
Tāraka, the deliverer [with] the form of the unchanging spirit of *sat-cit-ānanda* [of] Brahman [is] at the eyebrow centre. Seeing through the three points of concentration [is] the way to it. *Suṣumnā*, [which goes] from *mūlādhāra* up to

brahmarandhra [is] as bright as the sun. In its centre [is] *kuṇḍalinī*, [bright] as crores of lightning [and] subtle [as] the fibrous root of a lotus. Destruction of *tamas* [is] there. Through insight into it, [there is] destruction of all sins.

Commentary
Tāraka is the deliverer from the mundane existence of the cycle of conception, birth, life and death to *sat-cit-ānanda*: existence-consciousness-bliss, the three integral parts of Brahman, the ever-expanding consciousness. Bliss is that which remains when all states of mind have been transcended. Tāraka is at the eyebrow centre, the trigger point for *ājñā cakra*, where iḍā, piṅgalā and suṣumnā nāḍīs intersect, and is also known as the third eye, representing intuition and inner pure awareness. Physically it is at the medulla oblongata at the top of the spinal column in the mid-brain, corresponding to the pineal gland.

The three points of concentration are *bahir-lakṣya*, external point, *madhya-lakṣya*, intermediate point, and *antar-lakṣya*, inner point. Georg Feuerstein defines them as 'visionary experiences'.[9] Swami Niranjanananda says they are the three levels of *dhāraṇā*, holding the mind at one point. The first level, bahir lakṣya, is 'an external aim which one should focus upon to achieve the state of concentration'. It has a twofold purpose: to deepen the state of concentration, and to activate the left and right *nāḍīs*, *iḍā* and *piṅgalā*.[10]

The second level, madhya lakṣya, is 'focussing the mind on the experience of space, by concentrating on the three regions of space within the physical body'. They are *cidākāśa*, the space of consciousness, experienced in the head from *viśuddhi* at the throat, to *ājñā* at the eyebrow centre to *sahasrāra* at the crown of the head; *hṛdayākāśa*, space of the heart experienced in the chest, from *maṇipura* at the navel, to *anāhata* at the heart, to *viśuddhi* at the throat; *daharākāśa*, space of lower regions from *mūlādhāra*, at the perineum in men and cervix in women, to *svādhiṣthāna* in the lumbar region at the base of the spinal column to *maṇipura* at the navel.[11]

The third level, antar lakṣya is concentration on *brahma nāḍī*, the innermost nāḍī or tube in *suṣumnā nāḍī*. Suṣumnā nāḍī is the central energy flow moving up the spine from *mūlādhāra* to *svadhiṣṭhāna* to *maṇipura* to *anāhata* to *viśuddhi* to *ājñā* to *sahasrāra*, visualising it as a blazing luminous thread, through which *kuṇḍalinī*, the divine cosmic energy, rises.[12] Swami Muktibodhananda in her book *Swara Yoga* describes it thus: 'The brahma nāḍī is so called as it is via this channel that the higher centres of consciousness are directly stimulated. When kuṇḍalinī śakti passes into this channel, transcendental experience starts to take place.'[13]

Tamaḥ-nivṛttiḥ, the destruction of darkness and ignorance, occurs there because when the light of *kuṇḍalinī*, which has risen through the *brahma nāḍī* to brahmarandhra, the crown of the head at sahasrāra, the colour of cidākāśa changes from the darkness of tamas to white, as if the whole head is filled with light. The vision of this light removes all past karmas.

Verses 7 to 12: Effects of Tāraka

तर्जन्यग्रोर्मीलितकर्णरन्ध्रद्वये फूत्कारशब्दो जायते ।
तत्र स्थिते मनसि चक्षुर्मध्यनीलज्योतिः पश्यति ।
एवं हृदयेऽपि ॥७॥
बहिर्लक्ष्यं तु नासाग्रे चतुःषडष्टदशद्वादशाङ्गुलीभिः
क्रमान्नीलद्युतिश्यामत्वासदृग्रक्तभङ्गींस्फुरत्पीतवर्णद्वयोपेतं
व्योमत्वं पश्यति स तु योगी ॥८॥
चलनदृष्टया व्योमभागवीक्षितुः पुरुशस्य दृष्टयग्रे ज्योतिर्मयूखा
वर्तन्ते ।
तद्दृष्टिः स्थिरा भवति ॥९॥
शीर्षोपरि द्वादशाङ्गुलिमानं ज्योतिः पश्यति तदाऽमृतत्वमेति
॥१०॥
मध्यलक्ष्यं तु प्रातश्चित्रादिवर्णसूर्यचन्द्रवह्निज्वाला
वलीवत्तद्विहीनान्तरिक्षवत्पश्यति ॥११॥
तदाकाराकारी भवति ॥१२॥

tarjanyagrormīlitakarṇarandhradvaye phūtkāraśabdo jāyate
tatra sthite manasi cakṣurmadhyanīlajyotiḥ paśyati
evaṃ hṛdaye'pi (7)
bahirlakṣyaṃ tu nāsāgre catuḥṣaḍaṣṭadaśadvādaśāṅgulībhiḥ
kramānnīladyutiśyāmatvāsadṛgraktabhaṅgīṃsphuratpītavar
ṇadvayopetaṃ vyomatvaṃ paśyati sa tu yogī (8)
calanadṛṣṭayā vyomabhāgavīkṣituḥ puruṣasya dṛṣṭayagre
jyotirmayūkhā vartante
taddṛṣṭiḥ sthirā bhavati (9)
śīrṣopari dvādaśāṅgulimānaṃ jyotiḥ paśyati
tadā'mṛtatvameti (10)
madhyalakṣyaṃ tu prātaścitrādivarṇasūryacandravahnijvālā
valīvattadvihīnāntarikṣavatpaśyati (11)
tadākārākārī bhavati (12)

Vocabulary

karṇa-randhra-dvaye: when the orifices of the two ears; *mīlita*: are closed; *tarjanī-agroḥ*: by the tips of the forefingers; *phūtkāra-śabdaḥ*: sound of blowing; *jāyate*: is produced; *manasi*: when the mind; *sthite*: is fixed; *tatra*: there; *paśyati*: it sees; *nīla-jyotiḥ*: blue light; *cakṣuḥ-madhya*: between the eyes; *evam*: thus; *hṛdaye api*: also in the heart; *bahiḥ-lakṣyam*: external object; *paśyati*: one sees; *nāsāgre*: at the nosetip; *catuḥ-ṣaḍ-aṣṭa-daśa-dvādaśa-aṅgulībhiḥ*: by four, six, eight, ten and twelve finger widths; *kramāt*: respectively; *nīla-dyuti*: bright blue; *vyomatvam*: like the sky; *śyāmat-vāsadṛk*: like a dark- coloured garment; *sphurat*: quivering; *rakta-bhaṅgīm*: red wave; *varṇa-dvaya*: two colours; *pīta*: yellow and orange; *upetam*: together; *tu sa yogī*: then he [is] a yogin.

calana-dṛṣṭayā: moving the eyes; *puruṣasya*: person; *īkṣituḥ*: sees; *vyoma-bhāgau*: two parts of the sky; *jyotiḥ-mayūkhāḥ*: rays of light; *vartante*: occur; *dṛṣṭayagre*: at the corner of the eyes; *tad*: then; *dṛṣṭiḥ*: vision; *bhavati*: becomes; *sthirā*: steady; *paśyati*: he sees; *jyotiḥ*: light; *dvādaśa-aṅgulimānam*: of twelve finger widths; *upari*: above; *śīrṣaḥ*: head; *tadā*: then; *eti*: he goes to; *amṛtatvam*: immortal state; *madhya-lakṣyam*: middle object; *paśyati*: he sees; *prātaḥ*: in the morning; *citra-ādi*: various bright; *varṇa*: colours; *sūrya-candra-vahni-jvālā*: sun, moon, fire and water; *vihīna . . vat*: as if separate from; *antarikṣa*: sky; *tad*: then; *bhavati*: he has; *ākārā-ākārī*: nature and appearance.

Translation

When the orifices of the two ears are closed by the tips of the forefingers, a sound of blowing is produced. When the mind is fixed there, it sees a blue light between the eyes, thus also in the heart. [When] one sees the external object at the nosetip, by four, six, eight, ten and twelve finger widths in succession, bright blue like the sky [then] like a dark-coloured garment, [then] quivering [like] a red wave, [and then] the two colours yellow and orange together, one [is] a yogin.

[When,] moving the eyes, a person sees two parts of the sky, rays of light occur at the corner of the eyes. Then his vision becomes steady. [When] he sees a light of twelve finger widths above his head, then he goes to the immortal state. [When] the object [is] in the middle, he sees in the morning folds of various bright colours of the sun, moon, fire and water as if separate from the sky. Then he has their nature and appearance.

Commentary

When the ears are closed the awareness is directed inwards, thus inducing a meditative state and a perception of the vibration of the subtle sound. This is a nāda yoga practice which is a practice of dhāraṇā, one-pointed concentration. The basis of sound is vibration, and vibration is the basis of creation, the first vibration being the mantra AUM.

The vision of a blue light indicates the awakening of iḍā nāḍī. Iḍā rises from the kanda at the base of the spine through the cakras on the left side of the body up to *ājñā cakra*, and is the passive, mental or lunar force. It is also called *cit śakti* as it controls our mental experiences and the four organs of the mind (*buddhi*, *manas*, *citta* and *ahaṃkāra*), as well as *manomaya koṣa*, the dimension of the mind, and *vijñānamaya koṣa*, the dimension of intuition. The blue light is also seen in *anāhata cakra*, in the region of the heart. It is a blue lotus, in the centre of which 'burns the *akhanda jyotir*, unflickering eternal flame, representing the *jīvātmā*, individual soul'.[14]

The text then describes the flow and colours of the *tattwas*, the five elements, which are controlled by the three *guṇas*, the qualities of the potential energy of nature, *prakṛti*, viz *tamas*, *rajas*, and *sattva*. David Frawley describes them thus:

‘Sattva is the power of harmony, balance, light and intelligence – the higher or spiritual potential. Rajas is the power of energy, action, change and movement – the intermediate or life potential. Tamas is the power of darkness, inertia, form and materiality – the lower or material potential.’[15]

All beings in the material world, whether sentient or insentient, are comprised of the same five elemental energies: earth, water, fire, air and ether, which are of the colour yellow, white, red, bluish grey and black respectively. Through concentration on an external point, the nosetip, awareness arises of the tattwas as they move and change colour. ‘The different colours which appear spontaneously within the ākāśa indicate the active tattwa. The earth and water elements correspond to tamas; the fire element corresponds to rajas, and the air and ether elements correspond to sattwa. As the colours are seen to mix and diffuse, the interplay of the gunas becomes more obvious at an objective level.’[16]

When the vision becomes fixed upward on the ether, the light of *sahasrāra cakra* at the crown of the head and twelve digits beyond is seen, thus transcending the limited individual self. When the vision is only six digits from sahasrāra, the colours of the sun, moon, fire and water are seen appearing spontaneously within the *ākāśa*. The yogin identifies with their inner nature.

In the *Bhagavad Gita*, Krishna says ‘The radiance of the sun, the moon and the fire that illuminates the world, all stem from me. I enter each world through my energy and sustain everything. I become the moon and cause all plants to flourish. I become the fire of digestion, residing in the bodies of all living beings. And then in accordance with the incoming and outgoing life air I digest the four kinds of food.’[17]

Verses 13 to 14: Final Effects of Tāraka

अभ्यासान्निर्विकारं गुणरहिताकाशं भवति ।
विस्फुरत्तारकाकारगाढतमोपमं पराकाशं भवति ।
कालानलसमं द्योतमानं महाकाशं भवति ।
सर्वोत्कृष्टपरमाद्वितीयप्रद्योतमानं तत्त्वाकाशं भवति ।
कोटिसूर्यप्रकाशसंकाशं सूर्याकाशं भवति ॥१३॥
एवमभ्यासात्तन्मयो भवति य एवं वेद ॥१४॥

abhyāsānnirvikāraṃ guṇarahitākāśaṃ bhavati
visphurattārakākāragāḍhatamopamaṃ parākāśaṃ bhavati
kālānalasamaṃ dyotamānaṃ mahākāśaṃ bhavati
sarvotkṛṣṭaparamādvitīyapradyotamānaṃ tattvākāśaṃ bhavati
koṭisūryaprakāśasaṃkāśaṃ sūryākāśaṃ bhavati (13)
evamabhyāsāttanmayo bhavati ya evaṃ veda (14)

Vocabulary

abhyāsāt: through practice; *bhavati*: he becomes; *nirvikāram ākāśam*: unchangeable *ākāśa*; *rahita*: free from; *guṇa*: attributes; *parā-ākāśam*: supreme ākāśa; *tamopamam*: removes darkness; *gāḍha*: deep; *kāra*: appearance; *visphurat-tāraka*: glittering star; *mahā-ākāśam*: great ākāśa; *dyotamānam*: luminous; *samam*: like; *kāla-anala*: fire of time; *tattva-ākāśam*: elemental ākāśa; *pradyotamānam*: radiant; *advitīya*: unique; *parama*: supreme; *sarva-utkṛṣṭa*: best of all; *sūrya-ākāśam*: solar ākāśa; *saṃkāśam*: appearing as; *prakāśa*: bright; *koṭi-sūrya*: crores of suns; *ya veda*: he who knows; *evam*: thus; *abhyāsāt*: through practice; *bhavati tanmayaḥ*: becomes absorbed in [them].

Translation

Through practice he becomes the unchangeable *ākāśa* free from attributes. He becomes the supreme ākāśa [which] removes deep darkness [by] the appearance [of] the glittering star. He becomes the great ākāśa luminous like the fire of time. He becomes the elemental ākāśa, radiant, unique, supreme, the best of all. He becomes the solar ākāśa, appearing as bright as crores of suns. He who knows thus, through practice thus becomes absorbed in [them].

Commentary

Paramahamsa Niranjanananda describes the *ākāśa* or ethers in his book *Yoga Darshan* as follows.

Nirvikāram ākāśam is also known as *guṇa rahita ākāśa, guṇa* meaning 'quality' or 'attribute', *rahita* 'without', and *ākāśa* 'space', just as Brahman or Puruṣa, being unchangeable and without qualities.

Paramākāśa, the supreme ākāśa, is a 'deep dark space with a twinkling star-like light'. This is the state of *śūnya*, nothingness or emptiness. It is the 'state of darkness prior to enlightenment' After this, there is just pure awareness, beyond the duality of the external and internal.

Mahākāśa, the great ākāśa, is as 'bright like the middle of the sun, which no eyes can see'. Here one is immersed in pure awareness 'like being in the centre of the sun, surrounded by brilliance and light'.

Tattvākāśa, the elemental space, is the essence from which the elements originate. 'In this space, the tattwas are existing in a dormant state . . . there is no activity . . . only perfect/absolute stillness.'

Sūryākāśa, the solar ākāśa, is the luminous space of the sun or the soul which is pure and untainted.' Sūrya means both 'sun' and 'soul' which is the internal, self-luminous principle and illumination. This space of sūrya or ātma is considered to be the source of light which is manifest in every visible and invisible object of creation. It is both seen and unseen. This space is a permanent reality and it is illumined by the tattwas or elements. It represents the pure for of the tattwas at the time of their creation.'[18]

Thus, by constant practice, he becomes entirely made of the 'five luminous-consciousness spaces'[19], *vyoma pañcaka.*

तृतीयः खण्डः
tṛtīyaḥ khaṇḍaḥ

Third Section

Verses 1 to 6: Twofold Yoga: Tāraka and Amanaska

तद्योगं च द्विधा विद्ध पूर्वोत्तरविभागतः ।
पूर्वं तु तारकं विद्यादमनस्कं तदुत्तरमिति ।
तारकं द्विधम् मूर्तिताराकममूर्तितारकमिति ।
यदिन्द्रियान्तं तन्मूर्तितारकम् ।
यद्भ्रूयुगातीतं तदमूर्तितारकमिति ।।१।।
उभयमपि मनोयुक्तमभ्यसेत् ।
मनोयुकतान्तरदृष्टिस्तारकप्रकाशाय भवति ।।२।।
भ्रूयुगमध्यबिले तेजस आविर्भावः ।
एतत्पूर्वतारकम् ।।३।।
उत्तरं त्वमनस्कम् ।
तालुमूलोर्ध्वभागे महज्ज्योतिर्विद्यते ।
तद्दर्शनादणिमादिसिद्धिः ।।४।।
लक्ष्येऽन्तर्बाह्यायां दृष्टौ निमेषोन्मेषवर्जितायां चेयं शाम्भवी मुद्रा भवति ।
सर्वतन्त्रेषु गोप्यमहाविद्या भवति ।
तज्ज्ञानेन संसारनिवृत्तिः ।
तत्पूजनं मोक्षफलदम् ।।५।।
अन्तर्लक्ष्यं जलज्ज्योतिःस्वरूपं भवति ।
महर्षिवेद्यं अन्तर्बाह्येन्द्रियैरदृश्यम् ।।६।।
tadyogaṃ ca dvidhā viddha pūrvottaravibhāgataḥ

pūrvaṃ tu tārakaṃ vidyādamanaskaṃ taduttaramiti
tārakaṃ dvividham mūrtitārakamamūrtitārakamiti
yadindriyāntaṃ tanmūrtitārakam
yadbhrūyugātītaṃ tadamūrtitārakamiti (1)
ubhayamapi manoyuktamabhyaset
manoyuktāntaradṛṣṭistārakaprakāśāya bhavati (2)
bhrūyugamadhyabile tejasa āvirbhāvaḥ
etatpūrvatārakam (3)
uttaraṃ tvamanaskam
tālumūlordhvabhāge mahajjyotirvidyate
taddarśanādaṇimādisiddhiḥ (4)
lakṣye'antarbāhyāyāṃ dṛṣṭau nimeṣonmeṣavarjitāyāṃ ceyaṃ
śāmbhavī mudrā bhavati
sarvatantreṣu gopyamahāvidyā bhavati
tajjñānena saṃsāranivṛttiḥ
tatpūjanaṃ mokṣaphaladam (5)
antarlakṣyaṃ jalajjyotiḥsvarūpaṃ bhavati
maharṣivedyaṃ antarbāhyendriyairadṛśyam (6)

Vocabulary

viddhi: know that; *dividhā*: twofold; *vibhāgataḥ*: equally into; *pūrva-uttara*: earlier and later; *pūrvam*: earlier; *vidyāt tārakam*: is known as *tārakam*; *uttaram-iti*: later is called; *amanaskam*: free from thought, *lit.* mindless; *dvividham*: of two kinds; *iti*: there is; *mūrti-tārakam*: tāraka with form; *amūrti-tārakam*: tāraka without form; *yat*: that which; *indriya-antam*: ends with the senses; *bhrūyuga-atītam*: beyond both eyebrows; *abhyaset*: one should practise; *api*: also; *ubhayam*: both; *manaḥ-yuktam*: through the mind; *antara-dṛṣṭiḥ*: inner vision; *prakāśāya bhavati*: reveals; *tejasaḥ*: golden flame; *āvirbhāvaḥ*: appears; *bile*: in the cavern; *madhya*: between; *bhrūyugam*: two eyebrows; *etat*: this; *pūrva-tārakam*: earlier tāraka; *tu uttaraṃ amanaskam*: and the later [is] amanaska; *mahat-jyotiḥ*: great light; *vidyate*: is; *ūrdhvabhāge*: above; *tālu-mūla*: root of the palate; *tat-darśanāt*: through the sight of it; *siddhiḥ aṇima-ādi*: *siddhis* such as making the body small;

lakṣye: when the [spiritual] vision; *antaḥ*: internalised; *ca dṛṣṭau*: and the eyes; *bāhyāyām*: outward; *nimeṣonmeṣa-varjitāyām*: without blinking; *iyam bhavati*: this is; *mahā-vidyā*: great knowledge; *bhavati gopya*: is kept secret; *sarva-tantreṣu*: in all the tantras; *tat-jñānena*: through this knowledge; *saṃsāra-nivṛttiḥ*: *saṃsāra* ceases; *tat-pūjanam*: this practice; *mokṣa-phaladam*: gives the fruit of liberation; *antarlakṣyam*: inner object; *rūpam bhavati*: becomes; *jalat-jyotiḥ*: fluid light; *maharṣi-vedyam*: it is known by the great *ṛṣis*; *adṛśyam*: cannot be seen; *antaḥ-bāhya-indriyaiḥ*: through the internal and external senses.

Translation

Know that yoga [is] twofold, [divided] equally into earlier and later. The earlier is known as *tāraka*; the later is called *amanaska*. Tāraka [is] of two kinds. There is tāraka with form and tāraka without form. That which ends with the senses is tāraka with form. That which [is] beyond both eyebrows is tāraka without form. One should also practise both through the mind. The inner vision through the mind reveals tāraka. The golden flame appears in the cavern between the two eyebrows. This [is] the earlier tāraka. And the later [is] amanaska. The great light is above the root of the palate. Through the sight of it [arise] *siddhis*, such as making the body small. When the [spiritual] vision [is] internalised and the eyes [see] outward without blinking, this is *śāmbhavī mudrā*. [This] great knowledge is kept secret in all the *tantras*. Through this knowledge *saṃsāra* ceases. This practice gives the fruit of liberation. The inner object becomes fluid light. It is known by the great *ṛṣis* [and] cannot be seen through the internal and external senses.

Commentary

The practice of tāraka comes first and leads to amanaska, which can be translated as mindlessness, or transcendence of the thinking mind, when the mind is free from thought and desire.

The *Advaya-Tāraka-Upanishad* deals specifically with tāraka-yoga. Verse 10 says 'That Deliverer (Tāraka) is twofold: the Deliverer with form and the Deliverer without form. That which 'ends' with the senses is 'with form'. That which transcends the pair of eyebrows is 'without form'. In every case, in determining the inner import [of a thing] the application of a controlled mind is desirable.' Feuerstein says that 'the deliverer with form (*mūrti-tāraka*) which is in the range of the senses and consists in manifestations of light in the space between the eyebrows. The second type is the formless deliverer (*amūrti-tāraka*) which is the transcendental Light itself.'[20]

So Tāraka, the deliverer, is both with form and without form. When the mind wanders during meditative practice, then it needs
an external or internal object to focus on. Swami Niranjan says that

'this is because the mind naturally and spontaneously moulds itself around objects of perception. In everyday life, the mind does this continuously with various external objects and thoughts' He describes 'with form' as 'where one's awareness is fixed on a definite focal point or object, concentration takes place within the manifest dimension' and 'without form' as taking place 'within the unmanifest dimension'. He says that 'first of all, there must be intense meditation practice [with form] in order to purify the mind and make it one-pointed. One should eventually see the formless in all forms and all forms in the formless'.[21]

'Through regular practice, the distraction and dissipation of the mind gradually cease and the mind becomes stable. The mind is considered to be stable when the yogin can remain focussed within on one point without fluctuation for an extended duration.'[22] Regular continuous practice of tāraka eventually and spontaneously leads to the 'goal of this Yoga which is transmindedness (*amanaskatā*), the condition of living liberation (*jīvan-mukti*)'.[23]

When Tāraka transcends the pair of eyebrows, it is without form, and awakens *ājñā cakra*, expanding intuition and inner awareness. Swami Satyananda in his book *Kundalini Tantra* says that one 'who meditates on this awakened chakra sees a flaming lamp shining as the morning sun and dwells within the regions of fire, sun and moon'.[24]

Then when the mind is free of thought, the great light of the thousand-petalled lotus at the crown of the head, *sahasrāra*, is seen, and *siddhis* arise. Here siddhis refer to the eight powers of yogins who have practised regularly for a long time. They are reduction of physical size (*aṇimā*), reduction of weight (*laghimā*), effortless acquisition (*prāpti*), freedom of will (*prākāmya*), increase of size (*mahimā*), power of creation and destruction (*īśitvam*), control over everything (*vaśitva*) and increase of weight (*garimā*). The yogin views siddhis as obstacles on the spiritual path as his/her aim is nothing less than enlightenment while living in the physical body in this material world. Siddhis can be a temptation and distraction, preventing the yogin from attaining the goal of liberation in this lifetime.

Swami Vivekananda in his book *Raja Yoga* says that 'when the yogin has seen all these wonderful powers, and rejected them, he reaches the goal. What are all these powers? Simply manifestations. They are no better than dreams. Even omnipotence is a dream. It depends on the mind. So long as there is a mind it can be understood, but the goal is beyond even the mind.'[25]

Śāmbhavī mudrā (Shambhu's seal) is 'gazing at the spot between the eyebrows while inwardly contemplating the transcendental Self; Shambu, another name for God Shiva, and the yogin who has mastered this technique is said to resemble the great God himself.'[26]

Swami Niranjan says 'This practice is also known as *brūmadhya dṛṣṭi*, which means 'eyebrow centre gazing'. By this practice ājñā cakra is awakened, which enables one to transcend the fetter of the individual ego and to see the significance and the essence behind all manifest things'[27] and establish oneself in higher consciousness.

चतुर्थः खण्डः
caturthaḥ khaṇḍaḥ
Fourth Section

Verses 1 to 4: Inner Object at Sahasrāra

सहस्रारे जलज्ज्योतिरन्तर्लक्षम् ।
बुद्धिगुहायां सर्वाङ्गसुन्दरं पुरुषरूपमन्तर्लक्ष्यमित्यपरे ।
शीर्षान्तर्गतमण्डलमध्यगं पञ्चवक्त्रमुमासहायं नीलकण्ठं
प्रशान्तमन्तर्लक्ष्यमिति केचित् ।
अङ्गुष्ठमात्रः पुरुषोऽन्तर्लक्ष्यमित्येके ॥१॥
उक्तविकल्पं सर्वमात्मैव ।
तल्लक्ष्यं शुद्धात्मदृष्टया वा यः पश्यति स एव ब्रह्मनिष्ठो
भवति ॥२॥
जीवः पञ्चविंशकः स्वकल्पितचतुर्विंशान्तितत्त्वं परित्यज्य
षड्विंशः परमात्माहमिति निश्चयाज्जीवन्मुक्तो भवति ॥३॥
एवमन्तर्लक्ष्यदर्शनेन जीवन्मुक्तिदशायां स्वयमन्तर्लक्ष्यो भूत्वा
परमाकाशाखण्डमण्डलो भवति ॥४॥

sahasrāre jalajjyotirantarlakṣyam
buddhiguhāyāṃ sarvāṅgasundaraṃ
puruṣarūpamantarlakṣyamityapare
śīrṣāntargatamaṇḍalamadhyagaṃ
pañcavaktramumāsahāyaṃ nīlakaṇṭhaṃ
praśāntamantarlakṣyamiti kecit
aṅguṣṭhamātraḥ puruṣo'ntarlakṣyamityeke (1)
uktavikalpaṃ sarvamātmaiva
tallakṣyaṃ śuddhātmadṛṣṭāyā vā yaḥ paśyati sa eva
brahmaniṣṭho bhavati (2)
jīvaḥ pañcaviṃśakaḥ svakalpitacaturviṃśāntitattvaṃ
parityajya ṣaḍviṃśaḥ paramātmāhamiti niścayājjīvanmukto
bhavati (3)

evamantarlakṣyadarśanena jīvanmuktidaśāyāṃ svayamantarlakṣyo bhūtvā paramākāśākhaṇḍamaṇḍalo bhavati (4)

Vocabulary

antarlakṣyam: inner object; *sahasrāre*: at *sahasrāra*; *jalat-jyotiḥ*: fluid light; *apara iti*: others say; *puruṣa-rūpam*: form of *puruṣa*; *buddhi-guhāyām*: in the cave of the *buddhi*; *sundaram*: beautiful; *sarva-aṅga*: all limbs; *iti kecit*: some say; *praśāntam*: auspicious; *nīla-kaṇṭham*: blue-necked; *pañca-vaktram*: five-faced; *umā-sahāyam*: accompanied by Umā; *gam*: goes to; *maṇḍala-madhya*: centre of the sphere; *śīrṣa-antaḥ*: inside the head; *eke iti*: some say; *aṅguṣṭha-mātraḥ*: size of a thumb; *sarvam*: all; *vikalpam*: different perceptions; *ātma-eva*: the one *ātman*; *yaḥ paśyati*: whoever sees; *tat-lakṣyam*: meditation object; *dṛṣṭāyā*: from the viewpoint; *śuddha-ātma*: pure ātman; *sa eva*: he indeed; *bhavati*: becomes; *brahmaniṣṭhaḥ*: firmly established in Brahman.

jīvaḥ pañcaviṃśa-kaḥ: *jīva*, consisting of twenty-five parts; *parityajya*: having abandoned; *svakalpita*: self-made; *caturviṃśānti-tattvam*: twenty-four *tattvas*; *bhavati jivanmuktaḥ*: becomes a *jivanmukta*; *niścayāt*: through the conviction; *ṣaḍviṃśaḥ*: twenty-sixth; *iti paramātmā-aham*: is 'I am *paramātmā*'; *evam*: thus; *antarlakṣya-darśanena*: through the vision of the inner object of meditation; *bhūtvā*: having become; *svayam-antarlakṣyaḥ*: object of meditation oneself; *jīvanmukti-daśāyām*: while in the liberated state; *bhavati*: one becomes; *ākhaṇḍa-maṇḍalam*: indivisible sphere; *param-ākāśa*: transcendent ether.

Translation

The inner object [of concentration] at *sahasrāra* [is] fluid light. Others say the inner object [is] the form of *puruṣa* in the cave of the *buddhi*, beautiful [in] all his limbs. Some say the inner object [is] the auspicious blue-necked five-faced one, accompanied by Umā, [and which] goes to the centre of the sphere inside the head. Some say *puruṣa*, the size of a thumb, [is] the inner object. All [these], it is said, [are] the different perceptions of the one *ātman*. Whoever sees the meditation object from the viewpoint [of] the pure ātman, he indeed becomes firmly established in Brahman.

The *jīva*, consisting of twenty-five parts, having abandoned the self-made twenty-four *tattwas*, becomes a *jivanmukta* through the conviction [that] the twenty-sixth [tattwa] is 'I am *paramātmā*'. Thus, through the vision of the inner object of meditation, having become the object of meditation oneself, while in the liberated state, one becomes the indivisible sphere of the transcendent ether.

Commentary

According to the yogins, the ultimate or innermost focus is the liquid radiance at *sahasrāra*, the thousand-petalled centre of energy at the *brahmarandhra*, the opening at the crown of the head. According to the *vaiṣṇavas*, the innermost object is the form of the *puruṣa* (*lit.* 'who dwells in the body'), who is Viṣṇu or Narāyana, in the seat of the intellect. According to the *śaivas*, the innermost object is the blue-throated Śiva with five faces, who dwells in the halo of radiance in the head. Śiva's throat turned blue when he drank the poisons of the world, which remained in the throat without contaminating his system. The five faces relate to the five elements, the five senses and the five organs of the body. According to the *dahara vidyā*, which is the knowledge of Brahman residing in the lotus of the heart, the innermost object is *parabrahman* (the Supreme Brahman), also referred to as Purusa, *aṅgustha mātra* who is the size of a thumb. They are all symbols of the one *ātman*. To know this is to realise Brahman.

The *jīva* or *jīvātmā*, the individual or personal soul, is comprised of twenty-five causal, subtle and gross elements. The cause of the subtle and gross elements is *paramātmā*, which, the verse says, is the eternal unchangeable truth. One identifies only with that, when one no longer identifies with the subtle and gross elements that make up a human being. The subtle elements are *mahat*, the universal principle or intellect, *ahamkāra*, the principle of personal identity, *manas*, the thinking observant mind, and *citta*, memories and past impressions. From the ahamkāra come the five gross elements, each of which is divided into five. They are the *tanmātra*, the five senses of sound, touch, sight, taste and smell; the *pañca mahābhūta*, the five elements of ether, air, fire water and earth; the *jñānendriya*, the five organs of perception of ears, skin, eyes, tongue and nose; and the *karmendriya*, the five organs of action of vocal cords, hands, feet, genital organ and anus.

Once the jīva is detached from identification of the subtle and gross elements, one becomes a *jivanmukta*, liberated while embodied, knowing that one is *paramātmā.*

।।द्वितीयं ब्राह्मणम्।।

dvitīyaṃ brāhmaṇan

Second Brāhmaṇa

।।प्रथमः खण्डः।।

prathamaḥ khaṇḍaḥ

First Section

Verses 1 to 4: Antarlakṣya: Cause of All

अथ ह याज्ञवल्क्य आदित्यमण्डलपुरुषं पप्रच्छ ।
भगवन्नन्तर्लक्ष्यादिकं बहुधोक्तम् ।
मया तन्न ज्ञातम् ।
तद्ब्रूहि मह्यम् ।।१।।
तदा होवाच पञ्चभूतकारणं तडित्कूटाभं तद्वच्चतुःपीटम् ।
तन्मध्ये तत्त्वप्रकाशो भवति ।
सोऽतिगूढ अव्यक्तश्च ।।२।।
तज्ज्ञानप्लवाधिरूढेन ज्ञेयम् ।
तद्बाह्याभ्यन्तर्लक्ष्यम् ।।३।।
तन्मध्ये जगल्लीनम् ।
तन्नादबिन्दुकलातीतमखण्डमण्डलम् ।
तत्सगुणनिर्गुणस्वरूपम् ।
तद्वेत्ता विमुक्तः ।।४।।

atha ha yājñavalkya ādityamaṇḍalapuruṣaṃ papraccha
bhagavannantarlakṣyādikaṃ bahudhoktam
mayā tanna jñātam
tadbrūhi mahyam (1)

tadā hovāca pañcabhūtakāraṇaṃ taḍitkūṭābhaṃ
tadvaccatuḥpītam
tanmadhye tattvaprakāśo bhavati
so'tigūḍha avyaktaśca (2)
tajjñanaplavādhirūḍhena jñeyam
tadbāhyābhyantarlakṣyam (3)
tanmadhye jagallīnam
tannādabindukalātītamakhaṇḍamaṇḍalam
tatsaguṇanirguṇasvarūpam
tatvettā vimuktaḥ (4)

Vocabulary
atha: then; *yājñavalkya ha papraccha*: Yājñavalkya did ask; *puruṣam*: *puruṣa*, Supreme Being; *āditya-maṇḍala*: sphere of the sun; *bhagavan*: o Lord; *uktam*: has been described; *bahudhā ādikam*: has been described many times; *tat na jñātam*: it has not been understood; *mayā*: by me; *tat brūhi*: explain it; *mahyam*: for me; *tadā ha uvāca*: he did reply thus; *kāraṇam*: cause; *pañca-bhūta*: five elements; *bham*: lustre; *kūṭā*: many; *taḍit*: lightning; *tadvat*: likewise; *catuḥ-pītam*: four seats; *tat-madhye*: in the middle of that; *bhavati*: is; *tattva-prakāśaḥ*: light of its essence; *atigūḍha*: secret; *ca avyaktaḥ*: and subtle; *tat jñeyam*: this is to be known; *adhirūḍhena*: by embarking on; *jñāna-plava*: boat of wisdom; *tat-madhye*: in its midst; *jagat*: world; *līnam*: is absorbed; *akhaṇḍa-maṇḍalam*: indivisible sphere; *atītam*: beyond; *kalā*: potential; *bindu*: manifestation; *nāda*: inner sound; *svarūpam*: its form; *saguṇa-nirguṇa*: with and without qualities; *vettā tat*: knows this; *vimuktaḥ*: is liberated.

Translation
Then Yājñavalkya did ask the *puruṣa* in the sphere of the sun: "O Lord, *antarlakṣya* has been described many times before, [yet] it has not been understood by me. [Please] explain it for me." He did reply thus: "[It is] the cause of the five elements [and has] the lustre of many {flashes of] lightning, likewise its four seats. In the middle of that is the

light of its essence, secret and subtle. This is to be known by embarking on the boat of wisdom. The object of meditation is [both] external and internal. In its midst the world is absorbed. It [is] the indivisible sphere beyond the potential for the manifestation of the inner sound. Its form [is] with and without attributes. [Whoever] knows this is liberated.

Commentary

The *antarlakṣya*, whether it takes the form of the thousand-petalled lotus, Viṣṇu, Śiva or Parabrahman, is the universal lightning energy which is the cause of the five great elements (ether, air, fire, water and earth). The four seats refer to the manas, buddhi, citta and ahaṃkāra which are contained in the *antaḥkaraṇa*, the instrument of the mind.

Eventually, through meditation on an external or internal point, one gains *jñāna*, the highest spiritual wisdom. Brahman is the ever-expanding consciousness, the unmanifest transcendental unchangeable reality, which is constant and continuous, beyond sound, time and space. Whoever has a deep understanding of this is liberated.

Verse 5: Experiences of Śāmbhavī

आदावग्निमण्डलम् ।

तदुपरि सूर्यमण्डलम् ।

तन्मध्ये सुधाचन्द्रमण्डलम् ।

तन्मध्येऽखण्डब्रह्मतेजो मण्डलम् ।

तद्विद्युल्लेखावच्छुक्लभास्वरम् ।

तदेव शाम्भवीलक्षणम् ॥५॥

ādāvagnimaṇḍalam
tadupari sūryamaṇḍalam
tanmadhye sudhācandramaṇḍalam
tanmadhye 'khaṇḍabrahmatejo maṇḍalam
tadvidyullekhāvacchuklabhāsvaram
tadeva śāmbhavīlakṣaṇam (5)

Vocabulary
ādau: at first; *agni-maṇḍalam*: region of fire; *tat-upari*: above it; *sūrya-maṇḍalam*: region of the sun; *tat-madhye*: in its middle; *sudhā-candra-maṇḍalam*: region of the heavenly moon; *akhaṇḍa-brahma-tejaḥ*: indivisible radiance of the *brahman*; *tat bhāsvaram*: it [is] resplendent; *lekhāvat*: like a streak; *śukla*: white; *vidyut*: lightning; *tadeva*: that is; *lakṣaṇam*: sign.

Translation
At first the region of fire [is seen], above it the region of the sun, in its middle the region of the heavenly moon, [then] in its middle the region of the indivisible radiance of the *brahman*. It [is] resplendent like a streak [of] white lightning. That is the sign of *śāmbhavī*.

Commentary
Śāmbhavī means 'pertaining to Śambhu (Śiva). This powerful *mudrā*, eyebrow centre gazing, gives protection and

leads to *unmanī*, the state beyond the mind.

Paramahamsa Niranjanananda describes these different levels of experience of śāmbhavī in his book *Yoga Darshan.* They manifest as each stage of visualisation is perfected. The first is the region of fire where one concentrates on the whole body in the form of fire, as *agni-maṇḍala*. This is also a sensory experience, where the intense heat of the flames can be felt along the spine and the front of the body.

The second is on sun, which is visualised at the fixed point or symbol on which one is concentrating. The third concentration is on the moon, *candra-maṇḍala*, also called *ājñā-maṇḍala*, where the symbol of ājñā cakra is visualised. In the fourth concentration, the light at the centre of ājñā cakra is visualised. It is pure white light, neither hot nor cool. In the fifth concentration the lightning within the white light is visualised.[28]

Eventually the practitioner experiences a feeling of deep immutable peace.

David Frawley in his book *Vedic Yoga* quotes from the *Shukla Yajurveda*:

'That is Agni, That is the Sun, That is Vayu, and That is the Moon. That is the luminous, That is Brahman. These are the waters. He is the Lord of Creation.

All winkings of the eye were born of the Lightning Person (Vidyut Purusha). No one has grasped him, above, across, or in the middle.' Shukla Yajurveda XXXII.1

Here is his interpretation of this verse: 'In these *Yajurveda* verses, it is not just the outer Fire, Sun, Wind and Moon that are indicated, but both their inner and cosmic forms. That or

"Tat: is the Supreme Self. The Purusha is both the outer and the inner Fire, Sun, Wind and Moon and Waters. The lightning Purusha is the Vedic Indra who is the supreme Seer, with his Vajra or thunderbolt. In other words, the practice of Yoga is hidden in the very concept of the Vedic deities as powers of light and aspects of Yoga practice.'[29]

Verses 6 to 7: Three Views of Śāmbhavī

तद्दर्शने तिस्रो दृष्टयः अमा प्रतिपत् पूर्णिमा चेति ।
निमीलितदर्शनममादृष्टिः ।
अर्धोन्मीलितं प्रतिपत् ।
सर्वोन्मीलनं पूर्णिमा भवति ।
तासु पूर्णिमाभ्यासः कर्तव्यः ।।६।।
तल्लक्ष्यं नासाग्रम् ।
यदा तालुमूले गाढतमो दृश्यते ।
तदभ्यासादखण्डमण्डलाकारज्योतिर्दृश्यते ।
तदेव सच्चिदानन्दं ब्रह्म भवति ।।७।।

taddarśane tisro dṛṣṭayaḥ amā pratipat pūrṇimā ceti
nimīlitadarśanamamādṛṣṭiḥ
ardhonmīlitaṃ pratipat
sarvonmīlanaṃ pūrṇimā bhavati
tāsu pūrṇimābhyāsaḥ kartavyaḥ (6)
tallakṣyaṃ nāsāgram
yadā tālumūle gāḍhatamo dṛṣyate
tadabhyāsādakhaṇḍamaṇḍalākārajyotirdṛṣyate
tadeva saccidānandaṃ brahma bhavati (7)

Vocabulary

tat-darśane: upon seeing it; *iti*: there are; *tisraḥ*: three; *dṛṣṭayaḥ*: views; *amā*: *amā*, new moon; *pratipat*: *pratipat*, first phase; *pūrṇimā*: *pūrṇimā*, full moon; *amā-dṛṣṭiḥ*: sight of amā; *bhavati*: is; *darśanam*: looking; *nimīlita*: with closed eyes; *ardha-unmīlitam*: with half-opened eyes; *sarva-unmīlanam*: with fully-opened eyes; *tāsu*: of these; *pūrṇimā-abhyāsaḥ*: practice of pūrṇimā; *kartavyaḥ*: should be done; *tat-lakṣyam*: its focus; *nāsāgram*: nosetip; *yadā*: when; *gāḍha-tamaḥ*: deep darkness; *dṛṣyate*: is seen; *tālu-mūle*: at the root of the palate; *tat-abhyāsāt*: through this practice;

jyotiḥ: light; *ākāra*: form; *akhaṇḍa-maṇḍala*: indivisible sphere; *dṛṣyate*: is seen; *tadeva bhavati*: this alone is; *brahma*: *brahman*; *sat-cid-ānandam*: existence-consciousness-bliss.

Translation

Upon seeing it there are three views, *amā*, new moon, *pratipat*, first phase of the lunar fortnight, and *pūrṇimā* full moon. The sight of amā is looking with closed eyes, of pratipat with half-opened eyes, of pūrṇimā with fully-opened eyes. Of these the practice of pūrṇimā should be done. Its focus [is] the nosetip, when a deep darkness is seen at the root of the palate. Through this practice a light [of] the form [of] an indivisible sphere is seen. This alone is Brahman, *sat-cit-ānanda*.

Commentary

Śāmbhavī can be viewed with eyes closed (*amā*), eyes half-opened (*pratipat*) or eyes fully opened (*pūrṇimā*). These views are related to the phases of the moon, as the moon relates to the mind and meditation practices.

The verse says the practice of *pūrṇimā*, where the eyes are fully opened, is the most important. The point of concentration is the nosetip. At first a thick darkness is seen at the root of the palate. Then, by fixed concentration, a light like the form of an endless sphere can be seen. This is Brahman, the singular Absolute, *sat* (existence) *cit* (consciousness) *ānanda* (bliss), its three essential aspects.

Verses 8 to 10: Signs of Śāmbhavī

एवं सहजानन्दे यदा मनो लीयते तदा शाम्भवी भवति ।

तामेव खेचरीमाहुः ॥८॥

तदभ्यासान्मनःस्थैर्यम्

ततो बुद्धिस्थैर्यम् ॥९॥

तच्चिह्नानि आदौ तारकवद्दृश्यते ।

ततो वह्रदर्पणम् ।

तत उपरि पूर्णचन्द्रमण्डलम् ।

ततो नवरत्न प्रभामण्डलम् ।

ततो मध्याह्नार्कमण्डलम् ।

ततो वह्निशिखामण्डलं क्रमाद्दृश्यते ॥१०॥

evaṃ sjānande yadā mano līyate tadā śambhavī bhavati
tāmeva khecarīmāhuḥ (8)
tadabhyāsānmanaḥsthairyam
tato buddhisthairyam (9)
taccihnāni ādau tārakavaddṛśyate
tato vajradarpaṇam
tata upari pūrṇacandramaṇḍalam
tato navaratna prabhāmaṇḍalam
tato madhyāhnārkamaṇḍalam
tato vahniśikhāmaṇḍalam kramāddṛśyate (10)

Vocabulary

yadā: when; *manaḥ*: mind; *līyate*: is absorbed; *sahaja-ānande*: in innate bliss; *tadā*: then; *śambhavī bhavati*: *śambhavī* appears; *eva āhuḥ*: [that] alone is called; *tām khecarī*: the *khecarī*; *tat-abhyāsāt*: through its practice; *manaḥ-sthairyam*: firmness of the mind; *tataḥ*: then; *buddhi-sthairyam*: firmness of the intellect; *tat-cihnāni*: its signs; *ādau*: first; *dṛśyate*: it is seen; *tārakavat*: like a star; *tataḥ* then; *vajra*: diamond; *darpanam*: mirror; *pūrṇa-candra-maṇḍalam*: disc of the full moon; *upari*: above; *prabhāmaṇḍalam*: crown of rays; *navaratna*: nine gems; *maṇḍalam*: sphere; *madhyāhna-arka*: midday sun; *vahniśikhā-maṇḍalam*: circle of flames; *dṛśyate*: is seen; *kramāt*: in its turn.

Translation

When the mind is absorbed in its innate bliss, then *śambhavī* appears. That alone is called the *khecarī*. Through its practice [there is] firmness [of] the mind, then firmness of the intellect. [Here are] its signs: first it is seen like a star; then a diamond, a mirror; then the disc of the full moon above; then a crown of rays [with] nine gems; then the sphere of the midday sun; then a circle of flames is seen in its turn.

Commentary

Śāmbhavī mudrā is also known as *vaiṣṇavī mudrā,* the mudrā of Viṣṇu, because it leads to the seat of Viṣṇu, the Supreme Consciousness.

The word khecarī comes from two roots: *khe*, meaning 'sky' and *carya*, meaning 'one who roams'. The yogi, who perfects khecarī, is considered to be liberated while living. He is able to roam freely in the space of consciousness, unaffected by the limitations and associations of the mind and the world. In this sense, khecarī is synonymous with *mokṣa,* because it bestows liberation on its practitioners.

The yogin seeks to attain Viṣṇu, the supreme consciousness, through the practices of yoga and meditation. In this sense, Viṣṇu, the supreme being, is the universal light, which is seen by those who travel the path of self-realisation or enlightenment. This light is whaat guides the seeker on his chosen path towards the true essence of himself and of all existence.

Through regular practice of *śāmbhavī mudrā*, the mind, and

thence the intellect, becomes firm and stable. Successive signs of *śāmbhavī* are the appearance of a star, a diamond, a mirror, the full moon, a crown of gems, the midday sun, and a ring of flames.

द्वितीयः खण्डः

dvitīyaḥ khaṇḍaḥ

Second Section

Verses 1 to 4: Praṇava

तदा पश्चिमाभिमुखप्रकाशः
स्फटिकधूम्रबिन्दुनादकलानक्षत्रखद्योतदीपनेत्रसुवर्णनवरत्नादिप्र
भा
दृश्यन्ते ।
तदेव प्रणवस्वरूपम् ॥१॥
प्राणापानयोरैक्यं कृत्वा धृतकुम्भको
नासाग्रदर्शनदृढभावनया द्विकराङ्गुलिभिः
षण्मुखीकरणेन प्रणवध्वनिं निशम्य मनस्तत्र लीनं भवति
॥२॥
तस्य न कर्मलेपः ।
रवेरुदयास्तमययोः किल कर्म कर्तव्यम् ।
एवंविधश्चिदादीत्यस्योदयास्तमयाभावात्सर्वकर्माभावः ॥३॥
शब्दकाललयेन दिवारात्र्यतीतो भूत्वा
सर्वपरिपूर्णज्ञानेनोन्मन्यवस्थावशेन ब्रमैक्यं भवति ।
उन्मन्या अमनस्कं भवति ॥४॥

tadā paścimābhimukhaprakāśaḥ
sphaṭikadhūmrabindunādakalānakṣatrakhadyotadīpa-
netrasuvarṇanavaratnādiprabhā dṛśyante
tadeva praṇavasvarūpam (1)
prāṇāpānayoraikyaṃ kṛtvā dhṛtakumbhako
nāsāgradarśanadṛḍhabhāvanayā dvikarāṅgulibhiḥ

ṣaṇmukhīkaraṇena praṇavadhvaniṃ niśamya manastatra līnaṃ bhavati (2)
tasya na karmalepaḥ
raverudayāstamayayoḥ kila karma kartavyam evaṃvidhaścidādītyasyodayāstamayābhāvātsarvakarmābhāvaḥ (3)
śabdakālalayena divārātryatīto bhūtvā sarvaparipūrṇajñānenonmanyavasthāvaśena brahmaikyaṃ bhavati
unmanyā amanaskaṃ bhavati (4)

Vocabulary

tadā: then; *prakāśaḥ*: light; *abhimukha*: directed towards; *paścima*: west; *prabhā*: glow; *sphaṭika*: crystal; *dhūmra*: smoke; *bindu*: *bindu*, point of manifestation; *nāda*: inner sound; *kalā*: *kalā*, subtle power; *nakṣatra*: star; *khadyota*: firefly; *dīpa*: lamp; *netra*: eye; *suvarṇa*: gold; *navaratna*: nine gems; *ādi*: etc; *dṛśyante*: are seen; *tadeva*: this alone; *praṇava-svarūpam*: true form of *praṇava*, primal sound vibration.

kṛtvā aikyam: having united; *prāṇa-apānayoḥ*: *prāṇa* and *apāna*; *dhṛta-kumbhakaḥ*: maintained breath retention; *dṛḍha-bhāvanayā*: with strong willpower; *nāsāgra-darśana*: concentrated on the nosetip; *ṣaṇmukhī-karaṇena*: by performing *ṣaṇmukhī*; *dvikara-aṅgulibhiḥ*: with the two forefingers; *niśamya*: hearing; *praṇava-dhvanim*: sound of praṇava; *manas*: mind; *bhavati līnam*: becomes absorbed; *tatra*: there; *tasya*: this person; *na karma-lepaḥ*: is not tainted with karma; *kila*: indeed; *kartavyam*: to be done; *udaya-astamayayoḥ*: at the rising and setting; *raveḥ*: of the sun; *evam*: thus; *vidhaḥ*: one who knows; *udayāstamayā*: rising and setting; *ādityasya*: of the sun; *cit*: pure consciousness; *bhāvāt*: from the heart; *abhāvaḥ*: absence; *sarva-karma*: all karma.

bhūtvā: having become; *divā-rātri-atītaḥ*: beyond day and night; *layena*: through the dissolution; *śabda-kāla*: sound and time; *bhavati*: he becomes; *brahm-aikyam*: one with Brahman; *vaśena*: through the power; *unmani-avasthā*: state beyond mind; *sarva-paripūrṇa-jñānena*: all-perfect wisom; *unmanyā*: through mindlessness; *bhavati*: there is; *amanaskam*: freedom from thought.

Translation

Then [comes] the light directed towards the west [where] the glow of crystal, smoke, *bindu*, inner sound, *kalā*, star, firefly, lamp, eye, gold, nine gems etc are seen. This alone is the true form of *praṇava.*

Having united *prāṇa* and *apāna* [and] maintained breath retention, with strong willpower concentrated on the nosetip, [and] by performing *ṣaṇmukhī* with the two forefingers, hearing the sound of praṇava, the mind becomes absorbed there. This person is not tainted with *karma*. The karma [of rituals] is indeed to be done at the rising and setting of the sun. Thus [for] the one who knows [that] the rising and setting of the sun [of] pure consciousness [comes] from the heart, [there is] absence [of] all karma.

Having become [one who has gone] beyond day and night through the dissolution of sound and time, he becomes one with Brahman through the power [of] the state beyond mind, all-perfect wisdom. Through mindlessness there is freedom from thought.

Commentary

Then comes the light directed towards the west (the last birth before attaining liberation), the signs of which are the *bindu* (the point where the unmanifest becomes manifest), *kalā* (the potential of sound), *nāda* (the primal sound from which all creation has emerged) and the *navaratna* (the nine jewels representing the nine planets). Pervading these and the others, (crystal, smoke, star, firefly, lamp, eye, gold,) the light of pure consciousness can be seen.

The *Sanskrit Glossary of Yogic Terms* defines *praṇava* as the sacred syllable AUM, primal sound vibration [and] epithet of Visnu.[31]

'The *Śiva-Purāṇa* (1.17.4): *pra* from *prakṛti* (cosmos) and *nava* (boat), because *praṇava* is the boat by which the yogin can safely cross the ocean of existence and reach the shore of the Absolute.'[32]

Prāṇāyāma is the union of prāṇa and apāna, with a division of three kinds: exhalation, inhalation and retention. These three components are said to resonate with three sounds: inhalation 'A', retention 'U' and exhalation 'M'. These three sounds form the *praṇava, Aum.* Therefore, prāṇayama is formed by praṇava. Thus prāṇayama is praṇava.[33]

In *ṣaṇmukhī mudrā* the ears, eyes, nostrils and lips are closed with the fingers to direct the senses and the mind inwards, and the eyes are closed with the forefingers. In this verse an abbreviated form of *ṣaṇmukhī* is used where only the ears are closed with the forefingers in order to hear the *nāda*, the inner sound of AUM. Concentration on the nosetip, *nāsikāgra dṛṣṭi*, is a mudrā (a channel of cosmic energy) which is a trigger point for *mūlādhāra cakra.*

'Whoever concentrates with the prāṇa at the nosetip, thereby stimulating mūlādhāra cakra, enters into *turīya*, the fourth state of consciousness beyond the three states of waking, dreaming and sleeping, and the *karma* (results) of wrong-doings from previous lives are destroyed.'[34]

There is only one ritual that the yogin whose mind is in Brahman should continue to do, and that is *nitya karma*, reciting the *gāyatrī mantra* while facing east at sunrise, the *sandhya* or junction which marks the transition from darkness to light and again while facing west at sunset, marking the transition from light to darkness. The yogin knows that he is not the doer of the action. It is from the *ātman* located in the heart that the sun of pure consciousness rises and sets.

'Having merged the sound in the light and raising the eyebrows a little brings forth unmanī. For yogins who have attained deep relaxation, time does not exist.' By abandoning knowledge of past present and future, the mind goes into dissolution. Then only Brahman remains.[35]

Verse 5: Rituals for Amanaska

तस्य निश्चिन्ता ध्यानम् । सर्वकर्मनिराकरणमावाहनम् ।
निश्चयज्ञमासनम् । उन्मनीभावः पाद्यम् ।
सदाऽमनस्कमर्घ्यम् । सदादीप्तिरपारामृतवृत्तिः स्नानम् ।
सर्वत्र भावना गन्धः । दृक्´स्वरूपावस्थानमक्षताः ।
चिदाप्तिः पुष्पम् । चिदग्निस्वरूपं दूपः ।
चिदादित्यस्वरूपं दीपः ।
परिपूर्णचन्द्रामृतरसस्यैकीकरणं नैवेद्यम् ।
निश्चलत्वं प्रदक्षिणम् । सोऽहंभावो नमस्कारः ।
मौनं स्तुतिः । सर्वसंतोषो विसर्जनमिति य एवं वेद ।।५।।

tasya niścintā dhyānam; sarvakarmanirākaraṇamāvāhanam
niścayajñānamāsanam; unmanībhāvaḥ pādyam
sadā'manaskamarghyam; sadādīptirapārāmṛtavṛttiḥ snānam
sarvatra bhāvanā gandhaḥ; dṛksvarūpāvasthānamakṣatāḥ
cidāptiḥ puṣpam; cidagnisvarūpaṃ dūpaḥ
cidādityasvarūpaṃ dīpaḥ
paripūrṇacandrāmṛtarasasyaikīkaraṇaṃ naivedyam
niścalatvaṃ pradakṣiṇam; so'haṃbhāvo namaskāraḥ
maunaṃ stutiḥ; sarvasaṃtoṣo visarjanamiti ya evaṃ veda (5)

Vocabulary

tasya: when there is; *niścintā*: firmness; *nirākaraṇam*: removal; *sarva-karma*: all actions; *āvāhanam*: invocation; *āsanam*: abiding in; *jñānam*: wisdom; *niścaya*: through conviction; *unmanī-bhāvaḥ*: state of mindlessness; *sadā*: always; *amanaskam*: mind is free from thought; *vṛttiḥ*: state; *sadā-dīptiḥ*: eternal light; *apāra-amṛta*: unlimited nectar; *bhāvanā*: application; *gandhaḥ*: *sandal* (a scent); *sarvatra*: everywhere; *avasthānam*: abiding in; *svarūpa*: one's true form; *dṛk*: spiritual eye; *cit-āptiḥ*: attaining pure consciousness; *puṣpam*: flower; *dhūpaḥ*: incense; *svarūpam*:

essential form; *cit-agni*: fire of consciousness; *dīpaḥ*: light; *cit-āditya*: sun of consciousness; *ekīkaraṇam*: uniting; *amṛtarasasya*: with the nectar; *paripūrṇacandra*: full moon; *niścalatvam*: motionless; *pradakṣiṇam*: circumambulating the deity during worship; *bhāvaḥ*: attitude; *so'ham*: I am That; *namaskāraḥ*: offering reverence; *maunam*: silence; *stutiḥ*: praise; *sarva-saṃtoṣaḥ*: contentment in all; *visarjanam*: concludes; *iti*: so says; *yaḥ*: whoever; *veda evam*: knows this.

Translation

When there is firmness [of mind], [there is] *dhyānam*. The removal [of] all actions [is] an invocation. [It is] abiding in wisdom through conviction. The state of mindlessness [is necessary for] *pādya*. *Arghya* [is done] always [when] the mind is free from thought. The state [of] eternal light [and] unlimited nectar [is] *snāna*. The application [of] *gandha* [is] everywhere. Abiding in one's true form [through] the spiritual eye [is] *akṣata*. Attaining pure consciousness [is worshipped with] flower. Incense [is] the essential form of the fire of consciousness. The lamp's light [is] the essential form of the sun of consciousness. Uniting with the nectar [of] the full moon [is] *naivedya*. Motionless [is] circumambulation. The attitude 'I am That' [is] offering reverence. Silence [is] praise. Contentment in all concludes [worship]. So says whoever knows this.

Commentary

Dhyāna is the seventh limb of the eightfold path of yoga. The first four are the outer limbs of *yama*, *niyama*, *āsana* and *prāṇamaya*. The next four are the inner limbs of *pratyāhāra*, *dhāraṇā*, *dhyāna* and *samādhi*. Pratyāhāra is withdrawal of the senses from the external world. Dhāraṇā is fixed concentration on one point. Dhyāna is then the spontaneous state of meditation. Samādhi is the transcendental state of consciousness, where there is the experience of oneness with all beings.

'*Āvāhanam* [is an] invocation using mantras so the deity

manifests during the time of worship.'[36] The aspirant must be in the meditative state, refraining from actions in the external world. If one is not in the state of dhyāna, the offerings will be ineffective.

The verse describes the ritual for worshipping the amanaska state. *Pādya* is the offering of water for washing the feet. *Arghya* is water offered at the time of worship. *Snāna* is water offered for bathing, flooding the body with the food of the gods. *Gandha* is the offering of sandal paste with the awareness that Brahman is everywhere. *Akṣata* means whole grain rice, usually mixed with the red *kuṅkumam*, yellow turmeric and other coloured powders, and then used in puja rituals to awaken knowledge of the spiritual Self. It has the ability to attract the vibrations of the five main deities Krishna, Siva, Ganesha, Durga and Rama. The form of the sun of consciousness is *dīpa* (a small lamp fueled with ghee, an offering to the deity). *Naivedya* is the offering of food to a deity. The mind is still and at peace as one walks clockwise and ceremoniously around the deity. *Mauna* is both outer and inner silence as the inner noise prevents one from connecting with the deity. *Visarjana* is the concluding act of worship where a murti (image of the deity) is immersed in water.

तृतीयः खण्डः

tṛtīyaḥ khaṇḍaḥ

Third Section

Verses 1 to 2: Freedom from Tripuṭī

एवं त्रिपुट्यां निरस्तायां निस्तरङ्गसमुद्रवन्निवातस्थितदीपवद-
चलसंपूर्णभावाभावविहीनकैवल्यज्योतिर्भवति ।।१।।
जाग्रन्निद्रान्तः परिज्ञानेन ब्रह्मविद्भवति ।।२।।

evaṃ tripuṭyāṃ nirastāyāṃ
nistaraṅgasamudravannivātasthitadīpavad-
acalasaṃpūrṇabhāvābhāvavihīnakaivalyajyotirbhavati (1)
jāgrannidrāntaḥ parijñānena brahmavidbhavati (2)

Vocabulary

tripuṭyām nirastāyām: when the *tripuṭī* are removed; *evam*: thus; *bhavati*: one becomes; *jyotiḥ*: light; *kaivalya*: final liberation; *vihīna*: free from; *bhava-abhāva*: existence and non-existence; *saṃpūrṇa*: whole; *acala*: immobile; *nistaraṅga-samudravat*: like a calm ocean; *sthita*: still; *dīpavat*: as a lamp; *nivāta*: without wind; *bhavati*: one becomes; *brahmavit*: knower of Brahman; *parijñānena*: through awareness; *jāgrat*: waking state; *nidrāntaḥ*: end of sleep.

Translation

When the *tripuṭī* are thus removed, one becomes the light of final liberation free from existence and non-existence, whole, immobile, like a calm ocean, [as] still as a lamp in a windless [place]. One becomes a knower of Brahman through awareness of the waking state to the end of sleep.

Commentary

The *tripuṭī* is the aggregate of agent, object, and action, as in meditator, meditation and meditating; thinker, thought and thinking. When one realises the unity of the three, that there is no division between the three, then one becomes the light of *kaivalya*, final liberation in the state of consciousness which is Brahman beyond duality, where all differences are unified. The yogin has this realisation at every moment and in every state, whether it be waking, dreaming or sleeping.

Verses 3 to 4: Suṣupti and Samādhi

सुषुप्तिसमाध्योर्मनोलयाविशेषोऽपि

महदस्त्युभयोर्भेदस्तमसि लीनत्वान्मुक्तिहेतुत्वाभावाच्च ।।३।।

समाधौ मृदिततमोविकारस्य

तदाकाराकारिताखण्डाकारवृत्त्यात्मकसाक्षिचैतन्ये

प्रपञ्चलयः संपद्यते प्रपञ्चस्य मनः कल्पितत्वात् ।।४।।

ततो भेदाभावात् कदाचिद्बहिर्गतेऽपि मिथ्यात्वभानात् ।

सकृद्विभातसदानन्दानुभवैकगोचरो ब्रह्मवित्तदैव भवात ।।५।।

suṣuptisamādhyormanolayāviśeṣo'pi
mahadastyubhayorbhedastamasi
līnatvānmuktihetutvābhāvācca (3)
samādhau mṛditatamovikārasya
tadākārākāritākhaṇḍākāravṛttyātmakasākṣicaitanye
prapañcalayaḥ saṃpadyate prapañcasya manaḥ kalpitatvāt (4)

Vocabulary

mahat aviśeṣaḥ: main similarity; *suṣupti-samādhyoḥ*: between deep sleep and *samādhi*; *asti*: is; *manolaya*: loss of consciousness; *ubhayoḥ*: in both; *ca*: and; *bhedaḥ*: difference; *abhāvāt*: absence; *mukti-hetutva*: cause of liberation; *līnatvāt tamasi*: concealed in tamas; *samādhau*: in samādhī; *mṛdita-tamaḥ*: crushed tamas; *vikārasya*: when . . . is transformed; *tadā*: then; *ākāra-vṛtti*: form of the mind; *ākāra-ākārita*: takes the form; *akhaṇḍa*: formless; *ātmaka*: having the nature of; *sākṣi-caitanye*: consciousness of the witness; *prapañca-layaḥ*: dissolution of the universe; *saṃpadyate*: is absorbed; *manaḥ*: mind; *kalpitatvāt*: presumed to exist; *prapañcasya*: as the manifestation of the whole world.

Translation

The main similarity between deep sleep and *samādhi* is the loss of consciousness in both, and the difference [is] the absence [of] the cause of liberation [as it is] concealed in *tamas*. In samādhi, when the crushed tamas is transformed, then the form of the mind takes the shape of the formless, having the nature of the consciousness of the witness, [in which] the dissolution of the universe is absorbed, the mind presumed to exist as the manifestation of the whole world.

Commentary

Swami Vivekananda, the foremost disciple of Sri Ramakrishna, explains in his book *Raja Yoga* the difference between *suṣupti* and *samādhi.* In deep sleep, one breathes and moves about 'without any accompanying feeling of ego; he is unconscious, and when he returns from his sleep, he is the same man who went into it. The sum total of the knowledge which he had before he went in to the sleep remains the same; it does not increase at all. No enlightenment comes. But when a man goes into *samādhi*, if he goes into it a fool, he comes out a sage. Therefore *samādhi* is the superconscious state.'[37]

In deep sleep, the *vṛttis*, mental modifications of the mind, are still present although one is not aware of them. Sleep rests in *tamas* (mental dullness and darkness), so liberation cannot be attained through it. In *nirvikalpa samādhi* there is total identification with *turīya*, the fourth state, the superconscious state where the vṛttis cease to exist, the mind is completely absorbed in Brahman and the *jīva*, the individual soul, becomes one with the individual spirit.

Verses 5 to 7: Becoming a Jīvanmukta

ततो भेदाभावात् कदाचिद्बहिर्गतेऽपि मिथ्यात्वभानात् ।
दकृद्विभातसदानन्दानुभवैकगोचरो ब्रह्मवित्तदैव भवति ॥५॥
तस्य संकल्पनाशः स्यात्तस्य मुक्तिः करे स्थिता ।
तस्माद्भावाभावौ परित्यज्य परमात्मध्यानेन मुक्तो भवति
॥६॥
पुनःपुनः सर्वावस्थासु ज्ञानज्ञेयौ ध्यानध्येयौ लक्ष्यालक्ष्ये
दृश्यादृश्ये चोहापोहादि परित्यज्य जीवन्मुक्तो भवेत् ।
य एवं वेद ॥७॥

tato bhedābhāvāt kadācidbahirgate'pi mithyātvabhānāt
sakṛdvibhātasadānandānubhavaikagocaro
brahmavittadaiva bhavati (5)
tasya saṃkalpanāśaḥ syāttasya muktiḥ kare sthitā
tasmādbhāvābhāvau parityajya paramātmadhyānena mukto
bhavati (6)
punaḥpunaḥ sarvāvasthāsu jñānajñeyau dhyānadhyeyau
lakṣyālakṣye dṛśyādṛśye cohāpohādi parityajya jīvanmukto
bhavet
ya evaṃ veda (7)

Vocabulary

tataḥ: therefore; *api*: even though; *kadācit*: sometimes; *bahiḥ-gate*: externalised; *bheda-abhāvāt*: because of the absence of difference; *mithyātva-bhānāt*: because of false perception; *brahmavit*: knower of Brahman; *bhavati eva*: is indeed; *gocaraḥ*: attains; *eka anubhava*: unique experience; *sat-ānanda*: true bliss; *vibhāta*: dawned; *sakṛt*: spontaneously; *muktiḥ*: liberation; *sthitā*: is firmly; *kare*: in the hand; *tasya*: of one; *tasya*: whose; *saṃkalpa*: volition; *syāt*: is; *nāśaḥ*: destroyed; *tasmāt*: thus; *parityajya*: abandoned; *bhava-abhāvau*: existence and non-existence;

muktaḥ bhavati: one is liberated; *dhyānena*: by meditating on; *paramātma*: Supreme Spirit.

parityajya: having relinquished; *punaḥpunaḥ*: again and again; *sarva-avasthāsu*: in all the states; *jñāna-jñeyau*: knowledge and what is to be known; *dhyana-dhyeyau*: meditation and what is to be meditated on; *lakṣya-alakṣye*: target and lack of target; *dṛśya-adṛśye*: visible and invisible; *ca-ūha-apoha-ādi*: and reasoning and argument and so forth; *bhavet*: one becomes; *jīvanmuktaḥ*: *jivanmukta*; *yaḥ*: whoever; *veda evam*: knows thus.

Translation

Therefore, even though [one has] sometimes externalised because of the absence of difference [and] false perception, the knower of Brahman is indeed the [one who] attains the unique experience of true bliss [which] dawned spontaneously. Liberation is firmly in the hand of one whose volition is destroyed. Having thus abandoned [ideas of] existence and non-existence, one is liberated by meditating on the Supreme Spirit.

Having relinquished again and again in all the states [of consciousness] knowledge and what is to be known, meditation and what is to be meditated on, the target and lack of target, the visible and invisible, and reasoning and argument and so forth, one becomes a *jīvanmukta*. Whoever knows thus [becomes a *jīvanmukta*].

Commentary

When there is an absence of desires and concerns with the dualities of the mundane world, in the states of waking, dreaming and sleeping, then without effort one becomes established in the bliss of the Supreme Spirit.

Thus the *jivanmukta* does not hide or escape from the world. Krishna describes how the *jivanmukta* lives in the world.

‘In the midst of suffering and happiness his mind is neither confused nor kindled. He who is free from desires, passions, fear and anger is said to be a sage of tranquil mind. One who is free from all material desires, who is neither delighted nor disturbed by joys or sorrows is the one who stands firm in wisdom.’[38]

‘He who has no hate, envy or egotism, who is gracious and compassionate, equable in the face of pain and pleasure, who is tolerant, self-controlled, firm in resolve and fixed in devotional practice and whose mind and intellect are fixed on me, is dear to me.’[39]

चतुर्थः खण्डः

caturthaḥ khaṇḍaḥ

Fourth Section

Verses 1 to 3: Five States of Consciousness

पञ्चावस्थाः जाग्रत्स्वप्नसुषुप्तितुरीयतुरीयातीताः ।।१।।
जाग्रति प्रवृत्तो जीवः प्रवृत्तिमार्गासक्तः ।
पापफलनरकादि मास्तु शुभकर्मफलस्वर्गमस्त्विति कङ्क्षते ।।२।।
एवं स एव स्वीकृतवैराग्यात्कर्मफलजन्माऽलं ।
संसारबन्धनमलमिति विमुक्त्यभिमुखो निवृत्तिमार्गप्रवृत्तो भवति ।।३।।

pañcāvasthāḥ jāgratsvapnasuṣuptiturīyaturīyātītāḥ (1)
jāgrati pravṛtto jīvaḥ pravṛttimārgāsaktaḥ
pāpaphalanarakādi māstu
śubhakarmaphalasvargamastviti kaṅkṣate (2)
evaṃ sa eva svīkṛtavairagyātkarmaphalajanmā'laṃ
saṃsārabandhanamalamiti vimuktyabhimukho
nivṛttimārgapravṛtto bhavati (3)

Vocabulary

pañca-avasthāḥ: five states; *jāgrat*: waking; *svapna*: dreaming; *suṣupti*: deep sleep; *turīya*: *turīya*, fourth state; *turīya-atītāḥ*: beyond *turīya*; *jīvaḥ*: *jīva*, individual soul; *pravṛttaḥ*: engaged in; *jāgrati*: in the waking state; *āsaktaḥ*: attached to; *pravṛtti-mārga*: worldly path; *kaṅkṣate*: longs for; *iti*: saying; *mā astu*: let [me] not have; *pāpa-phala*: fruit of wrongdoings; *naraka-ādi*: in hell etc; *astu*: let [me] have; *phala*: fruit; *śubha-karma*: auspicious actions; *svargam*: heaven.

saḥ evam eva: this very same person; *svīkṛta*: having taken; *vairagyāt*: aversion; *iti*: saying; *alam*: enough; *janmāḥ*: rebirths; *karma-phala*: fruits of karma; *bandhanam*: bondage; *saṃsāra*: cycle of birth, death and rebirth; *bhavati*: becomes; *pravṛttaḥ*: committed to; *nivṛtti-mārga*: path of introversion; *abhimukhaḥ*: approaching; *vimukti*: final emancipation.

Translation

The five states [of consciousness are] waking, dreaming, deep sleep, *turīya* and beyond *turīya*. The *jīva* [who is] engaged in the waking state [and] attached to the worldly path longs for [this], saying: 'let [me] not have the fruit of [my] wrongdoings in hell etc, let me have the fruit of my auspicious actions [in] heaven'.

This very same person, having taken an aversion [to mundane life], saying 'enough [of] rebirths [due to] the fruits of [my] actions, enough of bondage to the cycle of birth, death and rebirth,' becomes committed to the path of introversion, approaching final emancipation.

Commentary

We are usually only in one of the three states of consciousness or awareness, *viz* waking, dreaming or sleeping. The fourth state, *turīya*, which transcends those three states, is the outcome of *dhyāna*, meditation, the pure cosmic consciousness permeating all four states. There is a fifth state called *turīyātīta*. Once the yogin is fully aware of the four states of consciousness, he transcends the fourth state, ascending to Brahman at the crown of the head, and finally attains *turīya-atīta*, 'that which transcends the fourth' or 'seer of turīya', the condition of living liberation.[40]

Here the paths of *pravṛtti* and *nivṛtti* are described. The follower of the path of pravṛtti, 'path of activity' which is the path of extroversion, activity in the material world. It is 'the orientation of the person who does not renounce the world, which consequently leads to rebirth after rebirth punctuated by repeated deaths.' Nivṛtti is the path of introversion, 'path of cessation', 'the spiritual orientation of the yogin, who has renounced the world.'[41]

Swami Niranjananda, in his discourse on pravritti and nivritti defines them as 'pravṛtti, that which leads towards *vṛttis*, involvement and participation [and] nivṛtti becoming separate from that involvement.'[42] 'The path of pravritti leads towards the world and the path of nivritti leads towards transcendence. In the pravritti path, you are engrossed and involved in the experience of the senses and the sense objects, and every action in life is performed under the sway of the vrittis. There is lack of restraint and discipline, and everything is based on the whims of the mind. If the whims are not satisfied, there is pain, unhappiness and depression.
The basic requirement to be uplifted spiritually and internally for a person involved in this path is attainment of restraint and discipline, including restraint of speech, mind and the senses.'[43]

Tamas and rajas guide the pravritti path. Sattwa guides the nivritti path. Entanglement in vrittis increases tamas. Rajasic qualities manifest through development of more vrittis. Worldly life is rajasic and tamasic.[44]

Verse 4: Path to Liberation

स एव संसारणाय गुरुमाश्रित्य कामादि त्यक्त्वा
विहितकर्मचरन्साधनचतुष्टयसंपन्नो हृदयकमलमध्ये
भगवत्सत्तामात्रान्तर्लक्ष्यरूपमासाद्य सुषुप्त्यवस्थाया
मुक्तब्रह्मानन्दस्मृतिं लब्ध्वा एक एवाहमद्वितीयः
कंचित्कालमज्ञानवृत्त्या तदुभयनिवृत्त्या प्राज्ञ
इदानीमस्मीत्यहमेक एव स्थानभेदादावस्थाभेदस्य
परंतु नहि मदन्यदिति जातविवेकः शुद्धाद्वैतब्रह्माहमिति
भिदागन्धं निरस्य स्वान्तर्विजृम्भितभानुमण्डलध्यानतदा-
काराकारितपरंब्रह्माकारितमुक्तिमार्गमारूढः परिपक्वो भवाति
॥४॥

sa eva saṃsāraṇāya gurumāśritya kāmādi tyaktvā vihitakarmacaransādhanacatuṣṭayasaṃpanno hṛdayakamalamadhye bhagavatsattāmātrāntarlakṣya-rūpamāsādya suṣuptyavasthāyā muktabrahmānandasmṛtiṃ labdhvā eka evāhamadvitīyaḥ kaṃcitkālamajñanavṛttyā vismṛtajāgradvāsanānuphalena taijaso'smīti tadubhayanivṛttyā prājña idānīmasmītyahameka eva sthānabhedādavasthābhedasya paraṃtu nahi madanyaditi jātavivekaḥ śuddhādvaitabrahmāhamiti bhidāgandhaṃ nirasya svāntarvijṛmbhitabhānumaṇḍaladhyānatadākārākārita-paraṃbrahmākāritamuktimārgamārūḍhaḥ paripakvo bhavati (4)

Vocabulary
eva: thus; *saḥ*: he; *āśritya*: having recourse to; *guru*: spiritual teacher; *saṃsāraṇāya*: from the mundane world; *tyaktvā*: giving up; *kāma-ādi*: all sensory pleasures; *caran*: engaged in; *vihita-karma*: prescribed actions; *saṃpannaḥ*: engaged with; *sadhana-catuṣṭaya*: four *sādhanas*; *āsādya*: attaining;

hṛdaya-kamala-madhye: in the centre of the lotus of the heart; *sattāmātra*: reality; *antar-lakṣya*: inner vision; *rūpam*: form; *bhagavat*: Lord; *labdhvā*: evoking; *smṛtiṃ*: memory; *ānanda*: bliss; *mukta-brahma*: liberated brahman; *avasthāyā*: in the state; *suṣupti*: deep sleep; *aham eka*: I am one; *advitīyaḥ*: without a second; *vṛttyā*: because of the condition; *ajñana*: ignorance; *kaṃcit-kālam*: for some time; *anuphalena*: as a consequence of; *vismṛta*: forgetting; *vāsana*: impressions; *jāgrat*: waking state; *asmi*: I am; *taijasaḥ*: dreaming state; *nivṛttyā*: having left; *ubhaya*: both; *idānīm-asmi*: I am now; *eva*: only; *eka prājña*: one *prājña*; *iti nahi*: there is nothing; *anyat*: else; *param*: beyond; *mad*: me; *bhedasya*: I have different; *avasthā*: states; *bhedāt*: due to the difference; *sthāna*: place; *nirasya*: having cast out; *bhidā-gandhaṃ*: scent of distinction; *aham*: I; *jāta-vivekaḥ*: innate discrimination; *śuddha-advaita-brahma*: pure non-dual Brahman.

ārūḍhaḥ: having attained; *mukti-mārgam*: path of liberation; *ākārita*: nature of; *paraṃ-brahma*: transcendent Brahman; *tadākāra-ākārita*: assuming its form and appearance; *dhyāna*: meditating on; *bhānu-maṇḍala*: sphere of the sun; *vijṛmbhita*: manifested; *sva-antaḥ*: within himself; *bhavati*: he becomes; *paripakvaḥ*: ripe.

Translation

Thus he, having recourse to a spiritual teacher [in order to be liberated] from the mundane world, giving up all sensory pleasures, engaged in prescribed actions, endowed with the four *sādhanas*, attaining, in the centre of the lotus of the heart the reality [of] the inner vision [which is] the form [of] the Lord, evoking the memory [of] the bliss [of] the liberated brahman [experienced] in the state [of] deep sleep, 'I am one without a second. Because of the condition [of] ignorance for some time [and] as a consequence of forgetting the impressions [in my] waking state, I am [in] the dreaming state. Having left both [states] I am now only the one *prājña*.

There is nothing else beyond me [although] I have different states due to the difference [in] place. Having cast out the scent of distinction I, [who have] innate discrimination, [am] the pure non-dual Brahman.'

Having attained the path of liberation, [which is] the nature of the transcendent Brahman, [after] assuming its form and appearance by meditating on the sphere of the sun manifested within himself, he becomes ripe [for emancipation].

Commentary
A guru, spiritual teacher, is necessary to break the illusion of the identity with the individual self and the addiction to the pleasures of the senses and worldly life, fulfilling the duties prescribed by the guru. Guru is spoken of as 'one who removes the darkness'. Guru is thus the illumined one, for only light can remove darkness.

The four *sādhanas* are the four qualities necessary for spiritual progress: *viveka* (discrimination between the permanent and impermanent), *vairagya* (dispassion, letting go of desire for mundane enjoyments), *ṣaḍsampatti* (the six virtues of equanimity, self-control, sensory withdrawal, endurance, faith and constant concentration on reality) and *mumukṣutva* (intense desire for liberation).

The centre of the lotus of the heart is also called *hṛdayākāśa*, 'the space in the heart where purity resides', directly connected with that part of the brain which is responsible for all the creative sciences and fine arts.[45] The *Taittiriya Upaniṣad VI.1* describes it thus: 'The bright space, familiar to all, is in the heart. Within that the intelligent, immortal and radiant soul (Puruṣa) exists who is realized and worshipped through meditation and knowledge.'[46]

Prājña is defined as 'the seer who observes the state of deep sleep, an individual in the causal state.'[47] Swami

Niranjananda says prājña is the seer 'who is aware of the causal dimensions of consciousness'.[48] He says prājña means 'all-knowing', 'what is known', 'the causal state in which the seed of the tattwas, the elements, is being germinated', 'non-decaying, non-changing principle'.[49] Prājña in Verse 6 of the *Mandukyopaniṣad* is described as 'the Lord supreme, the knower supreme, the authority supreme, the source supreme, the creator and destroyer of all beings'.[50]

The Sun is both an outer and inner energy source, reflecting its light within our hearts. The *Śvetaśvatara Upaniṣad II.1-4* says the mind must be controlled and senses restrained 'to see the self-luminous, infinite light'.[51] 'The deity of the *gayatri mantra*, Savitri, represents the transformational power inherent in the Sun, not only to change night into day but also to take us beyond the darkness of the ego into the infinite light of the higher Self.'[52]

Verses 5 to 6: Mind: Cause of Bondage and Liberation

संकल्पादिकं मनो बन्धहेतुः ।
तद्युक्तं मनो मोक्षाय भवति ।।५।।
तद्वांश्चक्षुरादिबाह्यप्रपञ्चोपरतो विगतप्रपञ्चगन्धः
सर्वजगदात्मत्वेन पश्यंस्त्यक्ताहंकारो ब्रह्माहमस्मीति
चिन्तयन्निदं सर्वं यदयमात्मेति भावयन्कृत्यो भवति ।।६।।

saṃkalpādikaṃ mano bandhahetuḥ
tadviyuktaṃ mano mokṣāya bhavati (5)
tadvāṃścakṣurādibāhyaprapañcoparato
vigataprapañcagandhaḥ
sarvajagadātmatvena paśyaṃstyaktāhaṃkāro
brahmāhamasmīti
cintayannidaṃ sarvaṃ yadayamātmeti bhāvayankṛtakṛtyo
bhavati (6)

Vocabulary

manaḥ: mind; *saṃkalpa-ādikam*: volition and so on; *hetuḥ*: cause; *bandha*: bondage; *tad-viyuktam*: freed of these; *bhavati mokṣāya*: has liberation; *tadvān*: thus; *uparataḥ*: free from; *bāhya*: external; *prapañca*: visible world; *cakṣuḥ-ādi*: sight and other [senses]; *vigata*: away from; *gandha*: odour; *paśyan*: seeing; *sarva-jagat*: all worlds; *ātmatvena*: through the essence of the *ātman*; *tyakta*: having renounced; *ahaṃkāra*: individual self; *iti*: knowing; *brahma-aham-asmi*: I am Brahman; *cintayan*: considering; *sarvam idam*: all this; *ayam-ātmā*: this ātman; *bhāvayan*: becoming; *kṛtakṛtyaḥ*: one who has done his duty; *bhavati*: he becomes.

Translation

The mind, [with] its volition and so on, [is] the cause [of] bondage. The mind freed of these has liberation. Thus, free from the external visible world of sight and other [senses], away from its odour, seeing all worlds through the essence of the *ātman*, having renounced the individual self, knowing 'I am Brahman', considering all this [as] this ātman, becoming one who has done his duty, he becomes [liberated].

Commentary

The volition and so on refers to the desires, expectations, judgements, likes and dislikes, and vrittis which keep the mind in bondage the world of duality.

'That embodied soul is thought [to be] complete [when] freed from these faults: desire, anger, fear and also delusion, greed, pride, lust, birth and death, miserliness, grief, laziness, hunger, thirst, craving, shame, fear, sorrow, despair and exultation as well.'[53]

The faults are dormant in the worldly person, ready to be activated by reactions to events and situations in the mundane world. They are called *doṣa*, faults, because they prevent us from knowing the pure consciousness. They are the experiences of the self in the world of duality, the most fundamental being *janma*, birth, and *mṛtyu*, death, which are the inevitable outcomes of association with the body that is born, lives for a period of time, and then dies.

Swami Satyananda says in his introduction to the *Mandukyopaniṣad*:

'Atman is associated with the waking, the dreaming and the deep sleep states. Finally these states are merged in Turiya, the Ultimate Reality. Atman becomes identical with Brahman – the indivisible, the transcendent, the incomprehensible, the cessation of all phenomena, the blissful – when Atman, the Om, merges his Self in the Self and attains Self-realization, which is the Ultimate Reality.'[54]

पञ्चमः खण्डः

pañcamaḥ khaṇḍaḥ

Fifth Section

Verses 1 to 4: The Yogin as Brahman

सर्वपरिपूर्णतुरीयातीतब्रह्मभूतो योगी भवति ।
तं ब्रह्मेति स्तुवन्ति ॥१॥
सर्वलोकस्तुतिपात्रः सर्वदेशसंचारशीलः परमात्मगगने
बिन्दुं निक्षिप्य शुद्धाद्वैताजाड्यसहजामनस्कयोग-
निद्राखण्डानन्दपदानुवृत्त्या भवाति ॥२॥
तच्चानन्दसमुद्रमग्ना योगिनो भवन्ति ॥३॥
तदपेक्षया इन्द्रादयः स्वल्पानन्दाह ।
एवं प्राप्तानन्दः परमयोगी भवतीत्युपनिषत् ॥४॥

sarvaparipūrṇaturiyātītabrahmabhūto yogī bhavati
taṃ brahmeti stuvanti (1)
sarvalokastutipātraḥ sarvadeśasaṃcāraśīlaḥ
paramātmagagane binduṃ nikṣipya
śuddhādvaitājāḍyasahajāmanaskayoganidrā-
akhaṇḍānandapadānuvṛttyā bhavati (2)
taccānandasamudramagnā yogino bhavanti (3)
tadapekṣayā indrādayaḥ svalpānandāḥ
evaṃ prāptānandaḥ paramayogī bhavatītyupaniṣat (4)

Vocabulary

yogī: yogin; *bhavati*: is; *bhūtaḥ*: has become; *sarva-paripūrṇa*: all-complete; *turiyātīta-brahma*: transcendent Brahman; *stuvanti*: worship; *tam*: him; *brahma-iti*: as Brahman; *śīlaḥ*: virtuous one; *pātraḥ*: vessel; *stuti*: praise; *sarva-loka*: in the whole world; *saṃcāra*: wandering through; *sarva-deśa*: all countries; *nikṣipya*: having cast; *gagane*: into the ether; *param-ātma*: Supreme Consciousness; *anuvṛttyā*: following; *pada*: path; *akhaṇḍa-ānanda*: uninterrupted bliss; *śuddha*: pure; *advaita*: non-dual; *ajādya*: vital; *sahaja*: innate; *amanaska*: thoughtless state; *bhavati*: he becomes.

ca tat: and then; *yoginaḥ bhavati*: yogin becomes; *magnā*: immersed in; *ānanda-samudra*: ocean of bliss; *tat-apekṣayā*: compared with this; *ānandāḥ indra-ādayaḥ*: bliss of Indra and others; *svalpa*: minute; *evaṃ*: thus; *prāpta-ānandaḥ*: having attained [this] bliss; *bhavati parama-yogī*: he becomes the Supreme Yogin; *iti upaniṣat*: so says the *upaniṣad.*

Translation

The yogin is [one who] has become the all-complete transcendent Brahman. [People] worship him as Brahman. This virtuous one [becomes] a vessel [of] praise [in] the whole world, wandering through all countries, having cast his *bindu* into the ether [of] the Supreme Consciousness, following the path of the uninterrupted bliss of *yoga-nidrā* [produced by] the pure non-dual vital innate thoughtless state, he becomes [one with Brahman].

And then the yogin becomes immersed in the ocean of bliss. Compared with this, the bliss of Indra and others is minute. Thus having attained this bliss, he becomes the Supreme Yogin. So says the *upaniṣad.*

Commentary

Having transcended the fourth state, turīyātīta, and ascended to Brahman, the yogin becomes the Brahman and is recognised by all as such. Brahman literally means 'vast expanse', from the root *bṛh* 'to grow, expand', often translated as the Absolute, 'the supreme principle behind and above all the various deities, beings and worlds'.[55]

Bindu here means 'making the dissolution of the mind' by

'the yogic process of transcending the conventional mind, which revolves around the pivot of the ego-sense.'[56]

Swami Satyadharma, in her commentary on *Yoga Darshana Upaniṣad*, describes the yogin who has become Brahman. 'The yogi, who has purified the karmas and samskaras that reside in the individual consciousness, and illumined the supreme self within, attains the goal of spiritual evolution. With this attainment, the self immediately reaches the state of fullness, or maturity, and realises its own immortality. When the yogi remains absorbed in this state, the all-pervading, ever effusive, consciousness shines continually, without interruption, in the mind.

Hence, absorbed in samādhi in every situation, with the mind ever directed towards the Self, he does not see all beings as diverse or many, but as one continuum of creation, ever unfolding from and returning back to the source of Brahma. In this way, pure consciousness is attained, which is unaffected or dissipated by any worldly relations or situations.'[57]

तृतीयं ब्राह्मणम्
tṛtīyaṃ brāhmaṇam

Third Brāhmaṇa

प्रथमः खण्डः
prathamaḥ khaṇḍaḥ

First Section

Verses 1 to 2: Amanaska

याज्ञवल्क्यो महामुनिर्मण्डलपुरुषं पप्रच्छ
स्वामिन्नमनस्कलक्षणमुक्तमपि विस्मृतं
पुनस्तल्लक्षणं ब्रूहीति ।।१।।
तथेति मण्डलपुरुषोऽब्रवीत् ।
इदममनस्कमतिरहस्यम् ।
यज्ज्ञानेन कृतार्थो भवति तन्नित्यं शांभवीमुद्रान्वितं ।।२।।
yājñavalkyo mahāmunirmaṇḍalapuruṣaṃ papraccha
svāminnamanaskalakṣaṇamuktamapi vismṛtaṃ
punastallakṣaṇaṃ brūhīti (1)
tatheti maṇḍalapuruṣo'bravīt
idamamanaskamatirahasyam
yajñānena kṛtārtho bhavati tannityaṃ śāṃbhavīmudrānvitam (2)

Vocabulary
mahā-muniḥ yājñavalkyaḥ: great sage Yājñavalkya; *papraccha*: asked; *maṇḍala-puruṣam*: *puruṣa* of the sphere; *svāmin*: o Master; *api*: although; *uktam*: I have been told; *amanaska-lakṣaṇam*: meaning of amanaska; *vismṛtam*: forgotten; *brūhi-iti*: please explain; *tat lakṣaṇam*: its meaning; *punaḥ*: again.

tathā: thus; *abravīt*: said; *idam-amanaskam*: this amanaska; *ati-rahasyam*: profound mystery; *ya-jñānena*: by knowing this; *bhavati*: one becomes; *kṛta-arthaḥ*: has fulfilled one's duties; *tat anvitam*: this is connected with; *nityam*: always.

Translation
The great sage Yājñavalkya asked the *puruṣa* of the sphere [of the sun]: 'o Master, although I have been told the meaning of amanaska, [I have] forgotten [it]. Please explain its meaning again'.

Thus the puruṣa of the sphere [of the sun] said: 'this amanaska is a profound mystery. By knowing this, one becomes [a person who] has fulfilled one's duties. This is always connected with *śāṃbhavī-mudrā'*.

Commentary
Once again Yājñavalkya asked the Supreme Being, who dwells in the Sun, Āditya, to explain the meaning of amanaska.

Śāmbhavī mudrā leads to amanaska. This is explained in the first Brāhmaṇa, third section, verses 5-6:
'When the [spiritual] vision [is] internalised and the eyes [see] outward without blinking, this is *śāmbhavī mudrā*. [This] great knowledge is kept secret in all the *tantras*. Through this knowledge *saṃsāra* ceases. This practice gives the fruit of liberation. The inner object becomes fluid light. It is known by the great *ṛṣis* [and] cannot be seen through the internal and external senses.' When *saṃsāra* ceases, there is amanaska, freedom from thought.

Verse 3: Contemplating the Paramātmā

परमात्मदृष्टया तत्प्रत्ययलक्ष्याणि दृष्ट्वा तदनु

सर्वशमप्रमेयमजं शिवं परमाकाशं निरालम्बमद्वयं

ब्रह्मविष्णुरुद्रादीनामेकलक्ष्यं सर्वकारणं परंब्रह्मात्मन्येव

पश्यमानो गुहाविहरणमेव निश्चयेन ज्ञात्वा

भावाभावादिद्वन्द्वातीतः

संविदितमनोन्मन्यनुभवस्तदनन्तरमखिलेन्द्रियक्षयवशादमनस्क

-सुखब्रह्मानन्दसमुद्रेमनः प्रवाहयोगरूपनिवातस्थितदीपवदचलं

परंब्रह्म प्राप्नोति ||३||

paramātmadṛṣṭyā tatpratyayalakṣyāṇi dṛṣṭvā tadanu sarvaśamaprameyamajaṃ śivaṃ paramākāśaṃ nirālambamadvayaṃ brahmaviṣṇurudrādīnāmekalakṣyaṃ sarvakāraṇaṃ paraṃbrahmātmanyeva paśyamāno guhāviharaṇameva niścayena jñātvā bhāvābhāvādidvandvātītaḥ saṃviditamanomanyanubhavastadanantaramakhilendriyakṣa ya-vaśādamanaskasukhabrahmānandasamudre manaḥ pravāhayogarūpanivātasthitadīpavadacalaṃ paraṃbrahma prāpnoti (3)

Vocabulary

dṛṣṭyā: by contemplating; *paramātma*: Supreme Self; *dṛṣṭvā*: seeing; *tadanu*: thereupon; *pratyaya-lakṣyāṇi*: aim of meditation; *sarvaśam*: whole; *aprameyam*: immeasurable; *śivam*: auspicious; *param-ākāśam*: transcendent ether; *nirālambam*: independent; *advayam*: non-dual; *eka-lakṣyam*: one goal; *brahma-viṣṇu-rudra-ādīnām*: Brahma Viṣṇu Rudra and others; *paśya*: seeing; *ātmani-eva*: in the one *ātman*; *paraṃ-brahma*: Supreme Reality; *sarva-kāraṇam*: cause of all; *niścayena*: without doubt; *jñātvā*: knowing; *viharaṇam*: roaming; *guhā*: cave; *dvandvātītaḥ*: free from the opposites;

bhāva-abhāva-ādi: existence and non-existence and others; *saṃvidita*: understanding; *anubhavaḥ*: experience; *mana-unmani*: *unmani* of the mind; *tadanantaram*: then; *vaśāt*: by living; *kṣaya*: without; *akhila*: all; *indriya*: senses; *prāpnoti*: one attains; *param-brahma*: Supreme Reality; *acalam*: motionless; *dīpavat*: like a lamp; *nivāta-sthita*: windless place; *yoga-rūpa*: form of merging; *pravāha*: river; *manaḥ*: of the mind; *brahma-ānanda-samudre*: with the ocean of the bliss of Brahman; *amanaska-sukha*: delight in the mindless state.

Translation

By contemplating the *paramātman* [and] seeing [that] thereupon [as] the aim of meditation whole, unborn, immeasurable, auspicious, the transcendent ether, independent, non-dual the one goal [of] Brahma, Viṣṇu, Rudra and others, seeing in the one *ātman* the Supreme Reality, the cause of all, without doubt knowing the roaming in the cave [of the heart], free from the opposites of existence and non-existence and others, understanding the experience [of] *unmani* of the mind, then by living without all the senses, one attains the Supreme Reality [which is] motionless like a lamp [in] a windless place, [taking] the form [of] merging with the river of the mind with the ocean of the bliss of Brahman [and] the delight in the mindless state.

Commentary

The verse describes the *paramātmā* and how the *jīvātmā*, the limited individual self, can attain liberation through meditation until one reaches the state between mind and thought, beyond the senses of sound, touch, sight, taste and smell, finally merging with the cosmic consciousness, transcendental supreme Self, *paramātmā*.

Swami Sivananda describes the superconscious state thus: 'the superconscious state, para-Brahman, [is that] where there are neither names nor forms, darkness nor light, east nor west, nor visible objects. It is the state of pure absolute consciousness. The goal of life is to attain this superconscious state. One has to transcend the body and mind to attain [it].'[58]

Verses 4 to 6: Undivided Bliss

ततः शुष्कवृष्कवन्मुर्रछानिद्रामय
निःश्वासोच्छ्वासाभावान्नष्टद्वन्द्वः
सदाऽचञ्चलगात्रः परमशान्तिं स्वीकृत्य मनःप्रचारशून्यं
परमात्मनि लीनं भवति ।।४।।
पयःस्नावानन्तरं धेनुस्तनक्षीरमिव सर्वेन्द्रियवर्गे
परिनष्टे मनोनाशो भवति तदेवामनस्कम् ।।५।।
तदनु नित्यशुद्धः परमात्माहमेवेति तत्त्वमसीत्युपदेशेन
त्वमेवाहमहमेव त्वमिति तारकयोगमार्गेणाखण्डानन्दपूर्णः
कृतार्थो भवति ।।६।।

tataḥ śuṣkavṛṣkavanmurchānidrāmaya niḥśvāsocchābhāvān-naṣṭadvandvaḥ sadā'cañcalagātraḥ paramaśāntiṃ svīkṛtya manaḥpracāraśūnyaṃ paramātmani līnaṃ bhavati (4)
payaḥsnāvānantaraṃ dhenustanakṣīramiva sarvendriyavarge
parinaṣṭe manonāśo bhavati tadevāmanaskam (5)
tadanu nityaśuddhaḥ paramātmāhameveti tattvamasītyupadeśena
tvamevāhamahameva tvamiti tārakayogamārgeṇākhaṇḍānandapūrṇaḥ
kṛtārtho bhavati (6)

Vocabulary

tataḥ: then; *śuṣka-vṛṣkavat*: like a dried-up tree; *dvandvaḥ*: dual; *maya*: consisting of; *murchā-nidrā*: lethargy and sleep; *naṣṭa*: lost; *abhāvāt*: through the absence of; *niḥśvāsa-utśvāsa*: exhalation and inhalation; *gātraḥ*: body; *sadā acañcala*: always steady; *svīkṛtya*: having acquired; *parama-śāntim*: absolute peace; *manaḥ*: mind; *śūnyam*: empty; *pracāra*: activity; *bhavati līnam*: one becomes dissolved;

paramātmani: in the Supreme Spirit; *tadeva*: only that; *amanaskam*: mindlessness.

tadanu: thereupon; *kṛta-arthaḥ*: having done one's duty; *bhavati*: one becomes; *nitya-śuddhaḥ*: ever pure; *tārakayoga-mārgeṇa*: through the path of *tāraka yoga*; *pūrṇaḥ*: full; *akhaṇḍa-ānanda*: undivided bliss; *iti*: thinking; *paramātmā-aham-eva*: I am the Supreme Spirit alone; *upadeśena*: implying; *tat-tvam-asi*: You are That; *tvam-eva-aham*: I am You alone'; *aham eva tvam*: You are I alone.

Translation
Then, like a dried-up tree, the dual [state] consisting of lethargy and sleep, lost through the absence of exhalation and inhalation, the body always steady, having acquired absolute peace, the mind empty [of] activity, one becomes dissolved in the Supreme Spirit. The destruction of the mind is when all groups of the senses are destroyed like the milk in the cow's udder after the glands [are emptied of] milk. Only that is mindlessness.

Thereupon, having done one's duty, one becomes ever pure, [and] through the path of *tāraka yoga*, full [of] undivided bliss, thinking 'I am the Supreme Spirit alone', implying 'You are That', 'You are I alone', 'I am You alone'.

Commentary
The dual state refers to the material mundane world where *tamas*, the *guna* (quality) of inertia, dullness and ignorance, is predominant. A dried-up tree refers to the destruction of the senses. Similarly, the cow's udder shrivels up after the milk has been drawn. It is this that is mindlessness.

Finally the yogin, who is now purified of worldly thoughts, has fulfilled his duty of attaining Self-realisation, the bliss of oneness with the Supreme Spirit.

In this state, says Swami Sivananda, the yogin 'feels that the Lord is sporting in all things as pure consciousness. He actually loses the sense of the material nature of things around him. Pure emotions rise in the heart and he begins to love every creature. He experiences the whole world as nothing but pure consciousness, and even tables, chairs, men, women and other things all appear to be made of this consciousness'.[59]

द्वितीयः खण्डः
dvitīyaḥ khaṇḍaḥ

Second Section

Verses 1 to 2: Becoming the Brahman

परिपूर्णपराकाशमग्नमनः प्राप्तोन्मन्यवस्थः
संन्यस्तसर्वेन्द्रियवर्गोऽनेकजन्मार्जितपुण्यपुञ्ज-
पक्वकैवल्यफलोऽखण्डानन्दनिरस्तसर्वक्लेशमलो
ब्रह्माहमस्मीति कृतकृत्यो भवति ।।१।।
त्वमेवाहं न भेदोऽस्ति पूर्णत्वात्परमात्मनः ।
इत्युच्चरन्त्समालिङ्ग्य शिष्यं ज्ञप्तिमनीनयत् ।।२।।
paripūrṇaparākāśamagnamanaḥ prāptonmanyavasthaḥ
saṃnyastasarvaendriyavargo'nekajanmārjitapuṇyapuñja-
pakvakaivalyaphalo'khaṇḍānandanirastasarvakleśakaśmalo
brahmāhamsmīti kṛtakṛtyo bhavati (1)
tvamevāhaṃ na bhedo'sti pūrṇatvātparamātmanaḥ
ityuccarantsamāliṅgya śiṣyaṃ jñaptimanīnayat (2)

Vocabulary
unmani-avasthaḥ: state of *unmani*; *prāpta*: having been attained; *manaḥ magna*: mind immersed in; *paripūrṇa*: fullness; *parākāśa*: Supreme Space; *vargaḥ*: group; *sarva-indriya*: all the senses; *saṃnyasta*: relinquished; *sarva-kleśa-kaśmalaḥ*: all sorrows and impurities; *nirasta*: dispelled; *akhaṇḍa-ānanda*: undivided bliss; *phalaḥ*: fruit; *puñja*: myriad; *puṇya*: merits; *aneka*: various; *janmāḥ-jita*: previous births; *pakva*: ripened; *kaivalya*: emancipation; *iti*: thinking; *brahma-aham-asmi*: I am Brahman; *bhavati*: becomes; *kṛta-kṛtyaḥ*: having fulfilled one's duty.

aham: I; *tvam eva*: you alone; *asti*: there is; *na bhedaḥ*: no difference; *pūrṇatvāt*: due to the fullness; *paramātmanaḥ*: of the Supreme Self; *uccarant iti*: saying thus; *samāliṅgya*: embracing dearly; *śiṣyam*: disciple; *anīnayat*: he brought to; *jñaptim*: understanding.

Translation

The state of *unmani* having been attained, the mind immersed in the fullness of the Supreme Space, the group of all the senses relinquished, [and] all sorrows and impurities dispelled, [now] in undivided bliss, the fruit [of] a myriad of merits [from] various previous births ripened [into] emancipation, thinking 'I am Brahman', [the yogin] becomes one who has fulfilled his duty.

'I am you alone.' There is no difference due to the fullness of the Supreme Self. Saying thus, dearly embracing his disciple [Yājñavalkya], he [the puruṣa] brought [him] to this understanding.

Commentary

Once the yogin is free of thought and is in the supreme void state of *parākāśa*, detached from the influence of the senses, all worldly mental activity abandoned, finally after many merits gained in previous lives, he has fulfilled his duty by reaching the ultimate goal, total liberation, knowing that he is Brahman, and Brahman alone.

So saying, the Lord of the Sun warmly embraced his disciple [Yājñavalkya], having led him to this realisation.

चतुर्थं ब्राह्मणम
caturthaṃ brāhmaṇam

Fourth Brāhmaṇa

Verses 1 to 5: The Five Ethers

अथ ह याज्ञवल्क्यो मण्डलपुरुषं पप्रच्छ
व्योमपञ्चकलक्षणं विस्तरेणानुब्रूहीति ॥१॥
स होवाचाकाशं पराकाशं महाकाशं ।
सूर्याकाशं परमाकाशमिति पञ्च भवन्ति ॥२॥
बाह्याभ्यन्तरमन्धकारमयमाकाशम् ।
बाह्यस्याभ्यन्तरे कालानलसदृशं पराकाशम् ।
सबाह्याभ्यन्तरेऽपरिमितद्युतिनिभं तत्त्वं महाकाशम् ।
सबाह्याभ्यन्तरे सूर्यनिभं सूर्याकाशम् ।
अनिर्वचनीयज्योतिः सर्वव्यापकं निरतिशयानन्दलक्षणं
परमाकाशम् ॥३॥
एवं तत्त्वल्लक्ष्यदर्शनात्तत्तद्रूपो भवति ॥४॥
नवचक्रं षडाधारं त्रिलक्ष्यं व्योमपञ्चकम् ।
सम्यगेतन्न जानाति स योगी नामतो भवेत् ॥५॥

atha ha yājñavalkyo maṇḍalapuruṣaṃ papraccha
vyomapañcakalakṣaṇaṃ vistareṇānubrūhīti (1)
sa hovācākāśaṃ parākāśaṃ mahākāśam
sūryākāśaṃ paramākāśamiti pañca bhavanti (2)
bāhyābhyantaramandhakāramayamākāśam
bāhyasyābhyantare kālānalasadṛśaṃ parākāśam
sabāhyābhyantare'parimitadyutinibhaṃ tattvaṃ mahākāśam
sabāhyābhyantare sūryanibhaṃ sūryākāśam
anirvacanīyajyotiḥ sarvavyāpakaṃ niratiśayānandalakṣaṇaṃ
paramākāśam (3)

evaṃ tattvallakṣyadarśanāttattadrūpo bhavati (4)
navacakraṃ ṣaḍādhāraṃ trilakṣyaṃ vyomapañcakam
samyagetanna jānāti sa yogī nāmato bhavet (5)

Vocabulary
atha ha: hence; *yājñavalkyaḥ papraccha*: Yājñavalkya asked; *maṇḍala-puruṣam*: Lord of the Sphere; *anubrūhi-iti*: please explain; *vistareṇa*: in detail; *pañcaka-lakṣaṇam*: fivefold kinds; *vyoma*: ether; *sa uvāca*: he replied; *iti*: thus; *bhavanti pañca*: there are five.

mayam: consists of; *bāhya-abhyantaram*: outer and inner; *andhakāra*: darkness; *sadṛśam*: like; *kālānala*: fire of all-destroying time; *bāhyasya-abhyantare*: of the outer and inner; *tattvam*: essence; *nibham*: like; *aparimita*: unlimited; *dyuti*: brilliance; *sa-bāhya-abhyantare*: that [which is] inner and outer; *sūrya-nibham*: resembles the sun; *jyotiḥ*: light; *anirvacanīya*: beyond description; *sarva-vyāpakam*: all-pervading; *lakṣaṇam*: nature; *niratiśaya-ānanda*: ultimate bliss; *evam*: thus; *darśanāt*: by concentration on; *tat-lakṣya*: its nature; *bhavati*: one becomes; *tat-rūpaḥ*: that form.

sa na jānāti: he does not know (*lit*); *samyak*: correct; *nava-cakram*: nine *cakras*: *ṣaḍ-ādhāram*: six *ādhāras*; *tri-lakṣyam*: three *lakṣyas*; *vyoma-pañcakam*: five *ākāśas*; *bhavet*: is; *yogī nāmataḥ*: yogin in name.

Translation
Hence Yājñavalkya asked the Lord of the Sphere [of the Sun]: 'please explain in detail the fivefold kinds [of] ether'. He replied thus: 'there are five [kinds of ether]: *ākāśa, parākāśa, mahākāśa, sūryākāśa* and *paramākāśa*.

Ākāśa consists of outer and inner darkness. Pārākāśa [is] like the fire of all-destroying time, [both] outer and inner. The essence of mahākāśa [is] like unlimited brilliance, [both] outer and inner. Sūryākāśa resembles the outer and inner sun.

Paramākāśa [is] the light beyond description, all-pervading [and of] the nature of ultimate bliss. Thus by concentration on its nature, one becomes that form.

Whoever does not have the correct knowledge of the nine *cakras*, six *ādhāras*, three *lakṣyas* [and] five *ākāśas* is a yogin in name [only].

Commentary
Verses I.2.13-14 have described the five kinds of ether. In these verses they are described as being both within the living person and in the outer atmosphere.

The yogin is one who has the experiential knowledge of the nine cakras (*mūlādhāra* at the perineum in men and cervix in women, *svādhiṣṭhāna* at the base of the spine in the lumbar region, *maṇipura* behind the navel in the spinal column, *anāhata* in the region of the heart, *viśuddhi* at the throat pit, *tālu* at the root of the palate, *ājñā* at the top of the spinal columan in mid-brain, *nirvāṇa* in the forehead and *sahasrāra* at the crown of the head), the six *ādhāras* (supports: arms, legs, spinal column, head, heart and anus), the three lakṣyas (points of concentration: outer, middle and inner), and the five ākāśas, subtle spaces as described in this verse and verses I:2:13-14. This verse declares that the ākāśas are both internal and external.

पञ्चमं ब्राह्मणम

pañcamaṃ brāhmaṇam

Fifth Brāhmaṇa

Verses 1 to 3: Dissolution of the Mind

सविषयं मनो बन्धाय निर्विषयं मुक्तये भवति ||१||

अतः सर्वं जगच्चित्तगोचरम् ।

तदेव चित्तं निराश्रयं मनोन्मन्यवस्थापरिपत्नं

लययोग्यं भवति ||२||

तल्लयं परिपूर्णे मयि समभ्यसेत्

मनोलयकारणमहमेव ||३||

saviṣayaṃ mano bandhāya nirviṣayaṃ muktaye bhavati (1)
ataḥ sarvaṃ jagaccittagocaram
tadeva cittaṃ nirāśrayaṃ manonmanyavasthāparipatnaṃ
layayogyaṃ bhavati (2)
tallayaṃ paripūrṇe mayi samabhyaset
manolayakāraṇamahameva (3)

Vocabulary

manaḥ: mind; *saviṣayam*: attached to sensual objects; *nirviṣayam*: not attached to sensual objects; *bhavati*: is, becomes; *muktaye*: liberated; *ataḥ*: thus; *sarvam*: all; *jagat*: world; *gocaram*: domain; *citta*: storehouse of the mind; *nirāśrayam*: independent; *paripatnam*: fully ripened; *unmani-avasthā*: *unmani* state; *manaḥ*: mind; *bhavati laya*: becomes dissolved; *yogam*: union; *samabhyaset*: one should practise; *tat-layam*: this dissolution; *mayi*: in me; *paripūrṇe*: completely full; *aham eva*: I alone; *kāraṇam*: cause; *manaḥ-laya*: dissolution of the mind.

Translation

The thinking mind attached to sensual objects is in bondage, [whereas the mind] not attached to sensual objects becomes liberated. Thus all the world [is in] the domain of *citta*, the storehouse of the mind. That citta, independent, fully ripened into the *unmani* state of the mind, becomes dissolved into union [with Brahman]. One should practise this dissolution in me [who am] completely full. I alone am the cause [of] the dissolution of the mind.

Commentary

The verses emphasise that attachment to sensual objects is enslavement of the mind. Therefore non-attachment to sensual objects is freedom of the mind. This is referred to as dissolution of the mind, which is called *nirvikalpa samādhi* in yoga.

Georg Feuerstein describes it thus. 'The unmanī state is the product of prolonged absorption in the formless ecstasy (*nirvikalpa samādhī*). This leads to dissolution of the mind (*mano-nāśa*), whereupon the transcendent Reality shines forth in its solitary majesty.' This is not 'wilful obliteration of one's rational faculties. . . it's the yogic process of transcending the conventional mind, which revolves around the pivot of the ego-sense.'[60]

Swami Sivananda defines nirvikalpa samādhi as 'that state in which one's identity with the universal reality is realized. When the mind ceases functioning, when all thoughts subside, when all consciousness of the body and the outer world is effaced from the mind, the individual soul completely merges into the supreme soul, into universal consciousness'. It is also known as the superconscious state, or turīya, the fourth state.[61]

Finally, the verse says that by meditating on the paramātman in the form of the *maṇḍalapuruṣa*, Lord of the Sun, the yogin can attain nirvikalpa samādhi.

Verses 4 to 5: Mind Dissolves in Viṣṇu

अनाहतस्य शब्दस्य तस्य शब्दस्य यो ध्वनिः ।

ध्वनेरन्तर्गतं ज्योतिर्ज्योतिरन्तर्गतं मनः ॥४॥

यन्मनस्त्रिजगत्सृष्टिस्थितिव्यसनकर्मकृत् ।

तन्मनो विलयं याति तद्विष्णो परमं पदम् ॥५॥

anāhatasya śabdasya tasya śabdasya yo dhvaniḥ
dhvanerantargataṃ jyotirjyotirantargataṃ manaḥ (4)
yanmanastrijagatsṛṣṭisthitivyasanakarmakṛt
tanmano vilayaṃ yāti tadviṣṇo paramaṃ padam (5)

Vocabulary
śabdasya: when a sound; *anāhatasya*: from the heart; *dhvaniḥ*: echo; *tasya śabdasya*: of that sound; *jyotiḥ*: light; *antargatam*: penetrating; *yat manaḥ*: which mind; *karmakṛt*: is the maker; *sṛṣṭi*: creation; *sthiti*: preservation; *vyasana*: destruction; *tri-jagat*: three worlds; *tat-manaḥ*: that mind; *yāti*: becomes; *vilayam*: dissolved in; *paramaṃ padam*: supreme seat; *viṣṇuḥ*: Viṣṇu.

Translation
When a sound [arises from] the heart, [there is] an echo of that sound, light penetrating the echo, the mind penetrating the light, which mind is the maker of creation, preservation [and] destruction of the three worlds. That mind becomes dissolved in the supreme seat of Viṣṇu.

Commentary
The heart here refers to the spiritual heart located in the region of the physical heart. It is the seat of the transcendental Self, and it is here where the subtle sound vibration of *aum* can be heard. It is the *śabda brahman,* the eternal sound which is the first manifestation of reality, seed of the Vedas.

Swami Satyananda in his book *Kundalini Tantra* describes aum as 'a sound which is non-physical and non-empirical, which is transcendental in nature, and this sound is endless and unbroken in the same way that the heart beats faithfully and continuously from before birth up until death'. The light refers to the *akhanda jyotir*, the steady motionless eternal flame, representing the jīvātma, individual soul.[62]

The three worlds can refer to the heaven, atmosphere and earth or heaven, earth and the lower world. 'Mind' refers to *mahat*, the greater mind, supreme intelligence. Viṣṇu is the Brahman, the preserver of the universe, the supreme consciousness.

Verses 6 to 8: Perfection of the Non-dual State

तल्लयाच्छुद्धाद्वैतसिद्धिर्भेदाभावात् ।
एतदेव परमतत्त्वम् ॥६॥
स तज्ज्ञो बालोन्मत्तपिशाचवज्जडवृत्त्या लोकमाचरेत् ॥७॥
एवममनस्काभ्यासेनैवनित्यतृप्तिरल्पमूत्रपुरीषमित
भोजनदृढाङ्गाजाड्यनिद्रादृग्वायुचलनाभावब्रह्म-
दर्शनाज्ञातसुखस्वरूपसिद्धिर्भवति ॥८॥

tallayācchuddhādvaitasiddhirbhedābhāvāt
etadeva paramatattvam (6)
sa tajjño bālonmattapiśācavajjaḍavṛttyā lokamācaret (7)
evamamanaskābhyāsenaivanityatṛptiralpamūtrapurīṣamita
bhojanadṛḍhāṅgājāḍyanidrādṛgvāyucalanābhāvabrahma-
darśanājñātasukhasvarūpasiddhirbhavati (8)

Vocabulary

tat-layāt: through this dissolution; *siddhiḥ*: perfection; *śuddha-advaita*: pure non-dual state; *abhāvāt*: due to the absence; *bheda*: division; *etat-eva*: this alone; *parama-tattvam*: highest truth; *saḥ tat-jñaḥ*: he who knows this; *ācaret*: behaves; *lokam*: world; *piśāca-vat*: like a demon; *unmatta*: madman; *bāla*: child; *vṛttyā*: in the manner; *jaḍa*: idiot.

evam: thus; *amanaska-abhyāsena*: through the practice of amanaska; *eva*: alone; *nitya-tṛptiḥ*: ever content; *alpa-mūtra-purīṣam*: little urine and faeces; *ita bhojana*: less food; *dṛḍhāṅga*: strong in body; *ajāḍya-nidrā*: without sluggishness or sleep; *dṛk-vāyu*: eyes and vital airs; *abhāva*: without; *calana*: movement; *ājñāta*: having realised; *brahma darśana*: vision of Brahman; *siddhiḥ-bhavati*: he attains; *svarūpa*: nature; *sukha*: bliss.

Translation

Through this dissolution [there is] the perfection of the pure non-dual state, due to the absence of division. This alone [is] the highest truth. He who knows this behaves in the world like a demon, madman [or] child in the manner [of] an idiot.

Thus through the practice of amanaska alone, ever content, [having] little urine and faeces [and] less food, strong in body, without sluggishness or sleep, eyes and vital airs without movement, having realised a vision of Brahman, he attains the nature of bliss.

Commentary

The yogin who has reached the non-dual egoless state should not expect or wish to be respected, praised or revered. Rather, he should appear to others like a fool, an idiot or a madman, and not react when he is treated thus.

'Liberation remains impossible within the confines of duality. Dual experience, the twofold nature, inherently causes struggle. The individual consciousness is mainly made up of ego, *ahamkara.* Due to the ego we are aware of dualities. Duality exists because of the ego. As long as there is duality there cannot be samādhi. As long as you remember yourself, you cannot get out of yourself.' 'When matter is transformed into light, matter is not seen, it is completely transformed.'[63]

Once the yogin has transcended the mind, he is always content, the body is pure, needing little food and excreting little, yet strong, vital and in a state of deep stillness and, seeing only Brahman, he attains the Supreme Bliss.

Verse 9: The Avadhūta

एवं चिरसमाधिजनितब्रह्मामृतपानपरायणोऽसै
संन्यासी परमहंस अवधूतो भवति ।
तद्दर्शनेन सकलं जगत्पवित्रं भवति ।
तत्सेवापरोऽपि मुक्तो भवति ।
तत्कुलमेकोत्तरशतं तारयति ।
तन्मातृपितृजायार्पत्यवर्गं च मुक्तं भवतीत्पनिषत् ।।९।।

evaṃ cirasamādhijanitabrahmāmṛtapānaparāyaṇo'sai
saṃnyāsī paramahaṃsa avadhūto bhavati
taddarśanena sakalaṃ jagatpavitraṃ bhavati
tatsevāparo'jño'pi mukto bhavati
tatkulamekottaraśataṃ tārayati
tanmātṛpitṛjāyārpatyavargaṃ ca muktaṃ bhavatītyupaniṣat
(9)

Vocabulary

evam: thus; *saṃnyāsī*: yogin; *pānaparāyaṇaḥ*: wholly intent on drinking; *brahma-amṛta*: nectar of the Brahman; *janita*: produced by; *cira-samādhi*: long [states of] *samādhi*; *bhavati*: becomes; *tat-darśanena*: by seeing this; *sakalam jagat*: the whole world; *bhavati pavitram*: becomes purified; *api ajñaḥ*: even an ignorant person; *tat-sevā-paraḥ*: intent on service to that; *bhavati muktaḥ*: becomes liberated; *tārayati*: he causes to cross to; *eka-śatam*: one hundred and one; *kulam*: family; *uttara*: north; *ca vargam*: and the whole; *mātṛ-pitṛ*: mother father; *jāyāḥ*: wife; *patya*: progeny; *bhavati muktam*: becomes liberated.

Translation

Thus the yogin, wholly intent on drinking the nectar of the Brahman produced by long [states of] transcendental awareness, becomes a *paramahaṃsa* [and] *avadhūta*. By seeing this the whole world becomes purified. Even an ignorant person intent on service to that becomes liberated. He causes one hundred and one [generations of his] family to cross to the north, and the whole [family], mother, father, wife, progeny becomes liberated.

Commentary

An *avadhūta* is 'one who is free from all worldly attachments or mental illusions'.[64]

'The yogin who has reached the lofty transmental state is called a supreme swan (*parama hamsa*) and an *avadhūta*, that is, one who has cast off everything.'[65] Dattātreya is a renowned example of an avadhūta.

'Avadhūta-Gītā [is] a late Vedantic work that describes and extols the life of the *avadhūta* who, in a blissful state of Self-realization, bows to no social convention but utterly renounces everything.'[66]

The verse says that anyone who, by purifying the mind, is dedicated to attaining samādhi in this lifetime, will be liberated and will cause a hundred and one generations of his family to cross the ocean of worldly existence.

इत्युपनिषत्

ityupaniṣat

Thus [ends] the upaniṣad.

APPENDICES

A. Notes

Advaya-Tāraka-Upaniṣad

1. The **Aparokshanubhuti** (**Sanskrit**: अपरोक्षानुभूतिः) is a famous work attributed to **Adi Shankara**. It is a popular introductory work (*prakran grantha*) that expounds **Advaita Vedanta** philosophy. It describes a method that seekers can follow to directly experience the essential truth of one's one nature. Thus, the work is literally titled Aparokshanubhuti, or Direct Experience. Swami Vimuktananda titles his translation Self-Realization.
2. Feuerstein, Georg *The Encyclopedia of Yoga and Tantra* (Shambala Publications, Boulder, USA 2011) p.205
3. Paramahamsa Niranjananda *Yoga Darshan* (Sri Panchdashnam Paramahamsa Alakh Bara 1993) p.173
4. Swami Satyananda Saraswati *Kundalini Tantra* (Bihar School of Yoga, Munger, Bihar, India 1996) p.148
5. *ibidem* p.149
6. Feuerstein, Georg *The Yoga Tradition* (Hohm Press, Prescott, Arizona, 2001) p.323
7. Swami Satyananda Saraswati *Asana Pranayama Mudra Bandha* (Bihar Yoga Bharati, Munger, Bihar, India) p.435

Maṇḍala-Brāhmaṇa-Upaniṣad

1. Frawley, David *Vedic Yoga: The Path of the Rishi* ((Lotus Press, Twin Lakes, Wisconsin 2014) p.234
2. Swami Satyadharma Saraswati *Yoga Darshana Upaniṣad* (2018) p.129 (translated by Ruth Perini) p.32 Vs.I.9-10
3. *ibidem* p.60 Vs.II.5b-6a
4. Swami Yogakanti *Sanskrit Glossary of Yogic Terms* (Yoga Publications Trust, Munger, Bihar, India 2007) p.88
5. Feuerstein, Georg *The Yoga-Sūtra of Patañjali* (Inner Traditions International, Vermont USA 1979) pp81-82 Vs.II.32
6. Swami Satyadharma Saraswati *Yoga Darshana Upaniṣad* (2018) p.129 (translated by Ruth Perini) p55 Vs.II.1-2a

7. Perini, Ruth *Trishikhi Brahmanopanishad* (2021) Vs.28b-32a commentary
8. Swami Satyadharma Saraswati *Yoga Tattwa Upanishad* (translated by Ruth Perini) (2nd edition 2018) Vs36b-38 commentary
9. Feuerstein, Georg *The Encyclopedia of Yoga and Tantra* (Shambala Publications, Boulder USA 2011) p.219
10. Paramahamsa Niranjanananda *Yoga Darshan* (Sri Panchdashnam Paramahamsa Alakh Bara 1993) p.165
11. *ibidem* p.167
12. *ibidem* p.171
13. Swami Muktibodhananda *Swara Yoga* (Satyananda Ashram, Mangrove Mountain NSW Australia 1983) p.32
14. Swami Satyananda Saraswati *Kundalini Tantra* (Bihar School of Yoga, Munger, Bihar, India 1996) p.149
15. Frawley, David *Vedic Yoga: The Path of the Rishi* ((Lotus Press, Twin Lakes, Wisconsin 2014) p.140
16. Paramahamsa Niranjanananda *Dharana Darshan* (Sri Panchdashnam Paramahamsa Alakh Bara 1993) p.321-322
17. *Bhagavad Gita* Srinivas Fine Arts Ltd (nightingale.co.in 2009) ch16vs12-14
18. Paramahamsa Niranjanananda *Yoga Darshan* (Sri Panchdashnam Paramahamsa Alakh Bara 1993) p168-170
19. Feuerstein, Georg *The Encyclopedia of Yoga and Tantra* (Shambala Publications, Boulder USA 2011) p.371
20. Feuerstein, Georg *The Yoga Tradition* (Hohm Press, Prescott, Arizona, 2001) p.322 & p.325
21. Paramahamsa Niranjanananda *Dharana Darshan* (Sri Panchdashnam Paramahamsa Alakh Bara 1993) p.25-28
22. Swami Satyadharma Saraswati *Yoga Tattwa Upanishad* (translated by Ruth Perini) (2nd edition 2018) Vs.73-75 commentary p.113
23. Feuerstein, Georg *The Encyclopedia of Yoga and Tantra* (Shambala Publications, Boulder, USA 2011) p.219
24. Swami Satyananda Saraswati *Kundalini Tantra* (Bihar School of Yoga, Munger, Bihar, India 1996) p.120
25. Swami Vivekananda *Raja Yoga* (Advaita Ashrama, Calcutta, India 1923) Vs.III.51 p.240

26. Feuerstein, Georg *The Yoga Tradition* (Hohm Press, Prescott, Arizona, 2001) p.396
27. Paramahamsa Niranjanananda *Yoga Darshan* (Sri Panchdashnam Paramahamsa Alakh Bara 1993) p.399
28. *ibidem* p.401
29. Frawley, David *Vedic Yoga: The Path of the Rishi* ((Lotus Press, Twin Lakes, Wisconsin 2014) p.116
30. Perini, Ruth *Shandilya Upanishad* (2020) Vs I.7.15 p.98-99
31. Swami Yogakanti *Sanskrit Glossary of Yogic Terms* (Yoga Publications Trust, Munger, Bihar, India 2007) p.138
32. Feuerstein, Georg *The Encyclopedia of Yoga and Tantra* (Shambala Publications, Boulder, USA 2011) pp.275-6
33. Perini, Ruth *Shandilya Upanishad* (2020) Vs.I.6.1-2
34. *ibidem* Vs.I.7.51
35. *ibidem* Vs.I.7.17-23
36. Swami Yogakanti *Sanskrit Glossary of Yogic Terms* (Yoga Publications Trust, Munger, Bihar, India 2007) p.30
37. Swami Vivekananda *Raja Yoga* (Advaita Ashrama, Calcutta India 1923) p.83
38. *Bhagavad Gita* Srinivas Fine Arts Ltd (nightingale.co.in 2009) II.56-57 pp128-9
39. *ibidem* XII.13-14 pp586-7
40. Perini, Ruth *Trishikhi Brahmanopanishad* (2021) Vs.149b-152a p129
41. Feuerstein, Georg *The Encyclopedia of Yoga and Tantra* (Shambala Publications, Boulder, USA 2011) pp.282 and 249
42. Swami Niranjanananda *The Paths of Pravritti & Nivrittti* (Yoga Publications Trust, Munger, Bihar, India 2011) p.13
43. *ibidem* p.33
44. *ibidem* p.20
45. Swami Satyananda Saraswati *Kundalini Tantra* (Bihar School of Yoga, Munger, Bihar, India 1996) p.148
46. Swami Satyananda Saraswati *Nine Principal Upanishads* (Yoga Publications Trust, Bihar 1975) p.221
47. Swami Yogakanti *Sanskrit Glossary of Yogic Terms* (Yoga Publications Trust, Munger, Bihar, India 2007) p.135
48. Paramahamsa Niranjanananda *Yoga Darshan* (Sri Panchdashnam Paramahamsa Alakh Bara 1993) p.242

49. *ibidem* p.245
50. Swami Satyananda Saraswati *Nine Principal Upanishads* (Yoga Publications Trust, Bihar 1975) p.54
51. *ibidem* pp170-1
52. Frawley, David *The Ancient Yoga of the Sun* (vedanet.com)
53. Swami Satyadharma Saraswati *Yoga Tattwa Upanishad* (translated by Ruth Perini) (2nd edition 2018) Vs.12-13 p.36
54. Swami Satyananda Saraswati *Nine Principal Upanishads* (Yoga Publications Trust, Bihar 1975) p.51
55. Feuerstein, Georg *The Encyclopedia of Yoga and Tantra* (Shambala Publications, Boulder, USA 2011) p.77
56. *ibidem* p.325
57. Swami Satyadharma Saraswati *Yoga Darshana Upaniṣad* (2018) p.129 (translated by Ruth Perini) Vs.6-12 p227
58. Swamis Sivananda & Satyananda *Maha Samadhi: Antardhyana* (Yoga Publications Trust, Munger, Bihar, India. 2010) p.55
59. *ibidem* p.56
60. Feuerstein, Georg *The Yoga Tradition* (Hohm Press, Prescott, Arizona, 2001) p.325
61. Swamis Sivananda & Satyananda *Maha Samadhi: Antardhyana* (Yoga Publications Trust, Munger, Bihar, India. 2010) p.26
62. Swami Satyananda Saraswati *Kundalini Tantra* (Bihar School of Yoga, Munger, Bihar, India 1996) pp.148-9
63. Swamis Sivananda & Satyananda *Maha Samadhi: Antardhyana* (Yoga Publications Trust, Munger, Bihar, India. 2010) p.179
64. Swami Yogakanti *Sanskrit Glossary of Yogic Terms* (Yoga Publications Trust, Munger, Bihar, India 2007) p.30
65. Feuerstein, Georg *The Yoga Tradition* (Hohm Press, Prescott, Arizona, 2001) p.325
66. Feuerstein, Georg *The Encyclopedia of Yoga and Tantra* (Shambala Publications, Boulder, USA 2011) p.54

B. References

Aiyar, K. Narayanasvami *Thirty Minor Upaniṣads* (Parimal Publications, Delhi India 2009)

Ayyaṅgār, T.R.Ś. *The Yoga Upaniṣads* (The Adyar Library 1938)

Bhagavad Gita Srinivas Fine Arts Ltd (nightingale.co.in 2009)

Feuerstein, Georg, **Kak** Subash & **Frawley** David *In Search of the Cradle of Civilization* (Quest Books, Illinois USA 2001)

Feuerstein, Georg *The Encyclopedia of Yoga and Tantra* (Shambala Publications, Boulder, USA 2011)

Feuerstein, Georg *The Yoga-Sūtra of Patañjali* (Inner Traditions International, Vermont USA 1979)

Feuerstein, Georg *The Yoga Tradition* (Hohm Press, Prescott, Arizona, 2001)

Frawley, David *The Ancient Yoga of the Sun* (vedanet.com)

Frawley, David *Gods, Sages and Kings* (Passage Press, Salt Lake City, Utah USA 1991)

Frawley, David *Vedic Yoga: The Path of the Rishi* ((Lotus

Press, Twin Lakes, Wisconsin 2014)

Joshi Bimali Trivedi *112 Upaniṣads* (Parimal Publications, Delhi India 2007)

Swami Niranjanananda *The Paths of Pravritti & Nivrittti* (Yoga Publications Trust, Munger, Bihar, India 2011)

Paramahamsa Niranjananda *Yoga Darshan* (Sri Panchdashnam Paramahamsa Alakh Bara 1993)

Paramahamsa Niranjanananda *Dharana Darshan* (Sri Panchdashnam Paramahamsa Alakh Bara 1993)

Perini, Ruth *Trishikhi Brahmanopanishad* (2021)

Perini, Ruth *Shandilya Upanishad* (2020)

Swami Muktibodhananda *Swara Yoga* (Satyananda Ashram, Mangrove Mountain NSW Australia 1983)

Swami Satyadharma Saraswati *Yoga Darshana Upaniṣad* (2018)

Swami Satyadharma Saraswati *Yoga Tattwa Upanishad* (2nd edition 2018)

Swami Satyananda Saraswati *Asana Pranayama Mudra Bandha* (Bihar Yoga Bharati, Munger, Bihar, India 1996)

Swami Satyananda Saraswati *Kundalini Tantra* (Bihar School of Yoga, Munger, Bihar, India 1996)

Swami Satyananda Saraswati *Nine Principal Upanishads* (Yoga Publications Trust, Bihar 1975

Swamis Sivananda & Satyananda *Maha Samadhi: Antardhyana* (Yoga Publications Trust, Munger, Bihar, India. 2010)

Swami Vivekananda *Raja Yoga* (Advaita Ashrama, Calcutta, India 1923)

Swami Yogakanti *Sanskrit Glossary of Yogic Terms* (Yoga Publications Trust, Munger, Bihar, India 2007)

C. Pronunciation Guide

a	nut
ā	father
i	bit
ī	knee
u	hook
ū	sue
ṛ	hurt
e	net
ai	time
o	got
au	house
ṃ	hum
ḥ	h + preceding vowel
k	paprika
kh	ink horn
g	ago
gh	big hut
ṅ	anger
c	chat
ch	much harm
j	jog
jh	raj house
ñ	engine
ṭ	borscht
ṭh	borscht home
ḍ	fresh dill
ḍh	flushed heart
ṇ	rainy
t	tarp
th	scout hall
d	modern
dh	mud hut

n	banal
p	papa
ph	top half
b	maybe
bh	mob hall
m	chroma
y	young
r	merit
l	alas
v	lava
ś	shin
ṣ	sunshine
h	hut

D. Sanskrit Text

अद्वयतारकोपनिषद्

।।शान्तिपाठः।।

ॐ पूर्णमिदः पूर्णमिदम् पूर्नापूर्णमुदच्यते ।
पूर्णस्य पूर्णमादाय पूर्णमेवावशिष्यते ।।
ॐ शान्तिः शान्तिः शान्तिः ।।

अथातोऽद्वयतारकोपनिषदं व्याख्यास्यामो यतये
जितेन्द्रियाय शमदमादिंषड्गुणपूर्णाय ।।१।।

चित्स्वरूपोऽहमिति सदा भावयन्त्सम्यङ् निमीलिताक्षः
किंचिदुन्मीलिताक्षो वान्तर्दृष्ट्या भ्रूदहरादुपरि
सच्चिन्नन्दतेजःकूटरूपं परम्ब्रह्मावलोकयंस्तद्रूपो भवति ।।२।।
गर्भजन्मजरामरणसंसारमहद्भयात्संतारयति तस्मात्तारकमिति ।
जीवेश्वरौ मायिकौ विज्ञाय सर्वविशेषं नेति नेतीति विहाय
यदवशिष्यते तदद्वयं ब्रह्म ।।३।।
तस्मिद्ध्यौ लक्ष्यत्रयानुम्संधानः कर्तव्यः ।।४।।

देहमध्ये ब्रह्मनाडी सुषुम्ना सूर्यरूपिणी पूर्णचन्द्राभा वर्तते ।
सा तु मूलाधारादारभ्य ब्रह्मरन्ध्रगामिनी भवति ।
तन्मध्ये ताडित्कोटिसमानकान्त्या मृणालसूत्रवत्सूक्षमाङ्गी
सूक्ष्माङ्गी कुण्डलिनीति प्रसिद्धास्ति ।
तां दृष्ट्वा मनसैव नरः सर्वपापविनाशद्वारा मुक्तो भवाति ।

फालोर्ध्वगललाटविशेषमण्डले निरन्तरं
तेजस्तारकयोगविस्फुरणेन
पश्यति चेत्सिद्धे भवति ।
तर्जन्यग्रान्मीलितकर्णरन्ध्रद्वये तत्र फूत्कारशब्दो जायते ।
तत्र स्थिते मनसि चक्षुर्मध्यगतनीलज्योतिःस्थलं
विलोक्यान्तर्दृष्ट्या निरतिशयसुखं प्राप्नोति ।
एवं हृदये पश्यति ।
एवमन्तर्लक्ष्यणं मुमुक्षुभिरुपास्यम् ।।५।।

अथ बहिर्लक्ष्यणं नासिकाग्रे चतुर्भिः
षद्भिरष्टभिर्दशभिर्द्वादशभिः क्रमादङ्गुलान्ते
नीलद्युतिश्यामत्वसदृग्रक्तभङ्गीस्फुरत्पीतशुक्लवर्ण-
द्वयोपेतव्योम यदि पश्यति स तु योगी भवति ।
चलदृष्ट्या व्योम भागवीक्षितुः पुरुषस्य दृष्ट्यग्रे
ज्योतिर्मयूखा वर्तन्ते ।
तद्दर्शनेन योगी भवति ।
तप्तकाञ्चनसंकाशज्योतिर्मयूखा अपाङ्गान्ते
भुमौ वा पश्यति तद्दृष्टिः स्थिरा भवति ।
शीर्षोपरि द्वादशाङ्गुलसमीक्षितुरमृतत्वं भवति ।
तत्र कुत्र स्थितस्य शिरसि व्योमज्योतिर्दृष्टं
चेत्स तु योगी भवाति ।।६।।

अथ मध्यलक्ष्यणं प्रातश्चित्रादिवर्णाखण्डसूर्यचक्रवद्वह्नि-
ज्वालावलीवत्तद्विहीनान्तरिक्षवत्पश्यति ।
तदाकाराकारितयावतिष्ठति ।

तद्भूयोदर्शनेन गुणरहिताकाशं भवति ।
विस्फुरत्तारकारसंदीप्यमानागाढतमोपमं परमाकाशं भवति ।
कालानलसमद्योतमानं महाकाशं भवति ।
सर्वोत्कृष्टपरमद्युतिप्रद्योतमानं तत्त्वाकाशं भवति ।
कोटिसूर्यप्रकाशवैभवसंकाशं सूर्याकाशं भवति ।
एवं बाह्याभ्यन्तरस्थव्योमपञ्चकं तारकलक्ष्यम् ।
तद्दर्शी विमुक्तफलस्तादृव्योमसमानो भवति ।
तस्मात्तारक एव लक्ष्यममनस्कफलप्रदं भवति ।।७।।
तत्तारकं द्विधं पूर्वार्धतारकमुत्तरार्धममनस्कं चेति ।
तदेष श्लोको भवति ।
तद्योगं च द्विधा विद्धि पूर्वोत्तरविधानतः ।
पूर्वं तु तारकं विद्यादमनस्कं तदुत्तरमिति ।।८।।

अक्ष्यन्तस्तारयोश्चन्द्रसूर्यप्रतिफलनं भवाति ।
तारकाभ्यां सूर्यचन्द्रमण्डलदर्शनं ब्रह्माण्डमिव
पिण्डाण्ड्शिरोमध्यस्थाकाशे रवीन्दुमण्डलद्वितयमस्तीति
निश्चित्य तारकाभ्यां तद्दर्शनमात्राण्युभयैक्यदृष्ट्या-
मनोयुक्तं ध्यायेत् ।
तद्योगाभावे इन्द्रियप्रवृत्तेरनवकाशात् ।
तस्मादन्तर्दृष्ट्या तारक एवानुसंधेयः ।।९।।

तत्तारकं द्विविधं मूर्तितारकममूर्तितारकं चेति ।
यदिन्द्रियान्तं तन्मूर्तिमत् ।
यद्भ्रूयुगातीतं तदमूर्तिमत् ।
सर्वत्रान्तःपदार्थविवेचने मनोयुक्ताभ्यास इष्यते तारकाभ्यां

सदूर्ध्वस्थ सत्त्वदर्शनान्मनोयुक्तेनान्तरीक्षणेन
सच्चिन्नन्दस्वरूपं ब्रह्मैव ।
तस्माच्छुक्लतेजोमयं ब्रह्मेति सिद्धम् ।
तद्ब्रह्म मनःसहकारिचक्षुषान्तर्दृष्ट्या वेद्यं भवति ।
वममूर्तितारकमपि मनोयुक्तेन चक्षुषैव दहरादिकं वेद्यं
भवति रूपग्रहणप्रयोजनस्य मनश्चक्षुरधीनत्वाद्बाह्यवदान्तरे-
ऽप्यात्ममनश्चक्षुःसंयोगेनैव रूपग्रहणकारयोदयात् ।
तस्मान्मनोयुक्तान्तर्दृष्टिस्तारकप्रकाशा भवति ।।१०।।

भ्रूयुगमध्यबिले दृष्टिं तदद्वारोर्ध्वस्थिततेज आविर्भूतं
तारकयोगो भवति ।
तेन सह मनोयुक्तं तारकं सुसंयोज्य प्रयत्नेन भ्रूयुग्मं
सावध्नानतया किंचिदूत्क्षेपयेत् ।
इति पूर्वभागी तारकयोगः ।
उत्तरं त्वमूर्तिमदमनस्कमित्युच्यते ।
तालुमूलोर्ध्यभागे महान् ज्योरिर्मयूखो वर्तते ।
तद्योगिभिर्ध्येयम् ।
तस्मादणिमादिसिसिद्धिर्भवति ।।११।।

अन्तर्बाह्यलक्ष्ये दृष्टौ निमेषोन्मेषवर्जितायां सत्यां
शांभवी मुद्रा भवति ।
तन्मुद्रारूढज्ञानिनिवसद्भूमिः पवित्रा भवति ।
तद्दृष्ट्वा सर्वे लोकाः पवित्रा भवन्ति ।
तादृशपरमयोगिपूजा यस्य लभ्यते सो'पि मुकतो भवति
।।१२।।

अन्तर्लक्ष्यजलज्योतिःस्वरूपं भवति ।
परमगुरूपदेशेन सहस्रारे जलज्योतिर्वा बुद्दहिगुहानिहितज्योतिर्वा
षोडशान्तस्थतुरीयचैतन्यं वान्तर्लक्ष्यं भवति ।
तद्दर्शनं सदाचार्यमूलम् ॥१३॥

आचार्यो वेदसम्पन्नो विष्णुभक्तो विमत्सरः ।
योगज्ञो योगनिष्ठश्च सदा योगात्मकः शुचिः ॥१४॥
गुरुभक्तिसमायुक्तः पुरुषज्ञो विशेषतः ।
एवं लक्षणसंपन्नो गुरुरित्यभिधीयते ॥१५॥
गुशब्दस्त्वन्धकातः स्याद्रुशब्दस्तन्निरोधकः ।
अन्धकारनिरोधित्वाद्गुरुरित्यभिधीयते ॥१६॥
गुरुरेव परं ब्रह्म गुरुरेव परा गतिः ।
गुरुरेव परा विद्या गुरुरेव परायणम् ॥१७॥
गुरुरेव परा काष्ठा गुरुरेव परं धनम् ।
यस्मात्तदुपदेष्टासौ तस्माद्गुरुतरो गुरुरिति ॥१८॥

यः सकृदुच्चारयति तस्य संसारमोक्षनं भवति ।
सर्वजन्मकृतं पापं तत्क्षणादेव नश्यति ।
सर्वान्कामानवाप्नोति ।
सर्वपुरुषार्थसिद्धिर्भवति ।
य एवं वेदेत्युपनिषत् ॥१९॥

॥ इति अद्वयतारकोपनिषत्समाप्ता ॥

मण्डलब्राह्मण उपनिषद्

।।शान्तिपाठः।।

ब्राह्मान्तस्तरकारं व्योमपञ्चकविग्र।
राजयोगैकसंसिद्धं रामचन्द्रमुपास्महे।।१।।
ॐ पूर्णमदः इति शान्तिः।

।।प्रथमं ब्राह्मणम्।।

।।प्रथमः खण्डः।।

याज्ञवल्क्यो ह वै महामुनिरादित्यलोकं जगाम ।
तमादित्यं नत्वा भो भगवन्नादित्यात्मतत्त्वमनुब्रूहीति ।।१।।

स होवाच नारायणः ।
ज्ञानयुक्तयमाद्यष्टाङ्गयोग उच्यते ।।२।।
शीतोष्णाहारनिद्राविजयः सर्वदा शान्तिर्निश्चलत्वं विषयेन्द्रियनिग्रहश्चैते यमाः ।।३।।

गुरुभक्तिः सत्यमर्गानुरक्तिः सुखागतवस्तवनुभवश्च तद्वस्त्वनुभवेन ।
तुष्टिर्निःसङ्गत्ता एकान्तवासो मनोनिवृत्तिः फलानभिलाषो वैराग्यभावश्च नियमाः ।।४।।
सुखासनवृत्तिश्चिरवासश्चैवमासननियमो भवति ।।५।।

पूरककुम्भकरेचकैः षोडशचतुःषष्टिद्वात्रिंशत्संख्यया यथाक्रमं प्राणायामः ।।६।।

विषयेभ्य इन्द्रियार्थेभ्यो मनोनिरोधनं प्रत्याहारः ।।७।।

विषयव्यावर्तनपूर्वकं चैतन्ये चेतःस्थापनं धारणं भवति ।।८।।

सर्वशरीरेषु चैतन्यैकतानता ध्यानम् ।।९।।

धयाहविस्मृतिःसमाधिः ।।१०।।

एवं सूक्ष्माङ्गानि ।

य एवं वेद स मुक्तिभाग्भवति ।।११।।

।।द्वितीयः खण्डः।।

देहस्य पञ्च दोषा भवन्ति कामक्रोधनिःश्वासभयनिद्राः ।।१।।

तन्निरासस्तु निःसंकल्पक्षमालघ्वाहाराप्रमादतातत्त्वसेवनम् ।।२।।

निद्राभयसरीसृपं हिंसादितरङ्गं तृष्णावर्तं दारपङ्कं संसारवार्धिं तरीतुं सूक्ष्ममार्गवलम्ब्य सत्त्वादिगुणानतिक्रम्य तारकमवलोकयेत् ।।३।।

भ्रूमध्ये सच्चिदानन्दतेजःकूटरूपं तारकं ब्रह्म ।।४।।

तदुपायं लक्ष्यत्रयावलोकनम् ।।५।।

मूलाधारादारब्य ब्रह्मरन्ध्रपर्यन्तं सुषुम्ना सूर्यभा ।

तन्मध्ये ताडत्कोटिसमा मृणालतन्तुसूक्ष्मा कुण्दलिनी ।

तत्र तमोनिवृत्तिः ।

तद्दर्शनात्सर्वपापनिवृत्तिः ।।६।।

तर्जन्यग्रोर्मीलितकर्णरन्ध्रद्वये फूत्कारशब्दो जायते ।
तत्र स्थिते मनसि चक्षुर्मध्यनीलज्योतिः पश्यति ।
एवं हृदयेऽपि ।।७।।
बहिर्लक्ष्यं तु नासाग्रे चतुःषडष्टदशद्वादशाङ्गुलीभिः
क्रमान्नीलद्युतिश्यामत्वासदृग्रक्तभङ्गींस्फुरत्पीतवर्णद्वयोपेतं
व्योमत्वं पश्यति स तु योगी ।।८।।
चलनदृष्टया व्योमभागवीक्षितुः पुरुशस्य दृष्टयग्रे ज्योतिर्मयूखा
वर्तन्ते ।
तद्दृष्टिः स्थिरा भवति ।।९।।
शीर्षोपरि द्वादशाङ्गुलिमानं ज्योतिः पश्यति तदाऽमृतत्वमेति
।।१०।।
मध्यलक्ष्यं तु प्रातश्चित्रादिवर्णसूर्यचन्द्रवह्निज्वाला
वलीवत्तद्विहीनान्तरिक्षवत्पश्यति ।।११।।
तदाकाराकारी भवति ।।१२।।

अभ्यासान्निर्विकारं गुणरहिताकाशं भवति ।
विस्फुरत्तारकाकारगाढतमोपमं पराकाशं भवति ।
कालानलसमं द्योतमानं महाकाशं भवति ।
सर्वोत्कृष्टपरमाद्वितीयप्रद्योतमानं तत्त्वाकाशं भवति ।
कोटिसूर्यप्रकाशसंकाशं सूर्याकाशं भवति ।।१३।।
एवमभ्यासात्तन्मयो भवति य एवं वेद ।।१४।।

तृतीयः खण्डः

तद्योगं च द्विधा विद्ध पूर्वोत्तरविभागतः ।
पूर्वं तु तारकं विद्यादमनस्कं तदुत्तरमिति ।
तारकं द्विधम् मूर्तितारकममूर्तितारकमिति ।
यदिन्द्रियान्तं तन्मूर्तितारकम् ।
यद्भ्रूयुगातीतं तदमूर्तितारकमिति ।।१।।
उभयमपि मनोयुक्तमभ्यसेत् ।
मनोयुकतान्तरदृष्टिस्तारकप्रकाशाय भवति ।।२।।
भ्रूयुगमध्यबिले तेजस आविर्भावः ।
एतत्पूर्वतारकम् ।।३।।
उत्तरं त्वमनस्कम् ।
तालुमूलोर्ध्वभागे महज्ज्योतिर्विद्यते ।
तद्दर्शनादणिमादिसिद्धिः ।।४।।
लक्ष्येऽन्तर्बाह्यायां दृष्टौ निमेषोन्मेषवर्जितायां चेयं शाम्भवी मुद्रा भवति ।
सर्वतन्त्रेषु गोप्यमहाविद्या भवति ।
तज्ज्ञानेन संसारनिवृत्तिः ।
तत्पूजनं मोक्षफलदम् ।।५।।
अन्तर्लक्ष्यं जलज्ज्योतिःस्वरूपं भवति ।
महर्षिवेद्यं अन्तर्बाह्येन्द्रियैरदृश्यम् ।।६।।

चतुर्थः खण्डः

सहस्रारे जलज्ज्योतिरन्तर्लक्षम् ।
बुद्धिगुहायां सर्वाङ्गसुन्दरं पुरुषरूपमन्तर्लक्ष्यमित्यपरे ।

शीर्षाम्तर्गतमण्डलमध्यगं पञ्चवक्त्रमुमासहायं नीलकण्ठं प्रशान्तमन्तर्लक्ष्यमिति केचित् ।
अङ्गुष्ठमात्रः पुरुषोऽन्तर्लक्ष्यमित्येके ॥१॥
उक्तविकल्पं सर्वमात्मैव ।
तल्लक्ष्यं शुद्धात्मदृष्टया वा यः पश्यति स एव ब्रह्मनिष्ठो भवति ॥२॥
जीवः पञ्चविंशकः स्वकल्पितचतुर्विंशान्तितत्त्वं परित्यज्य षड्विंशः परमात्माहमिति निश्चयाज्जीवन्मुक्तो भवति ॥३॥
एवमन्तर्लक्ष्यदर्शनेन जीवन्मुक्तिदशायां स्वयमन्तर्लक्ष्यो भूत्वा परमाकाशाखण्डमण्डलो भवति ॥४॥

॥द्वितीयं ब्राह्मणम्॥

॥प्रथमः खण्डः॥

अथ ह याज्ञवल्क्य आदित्यमण्डलपुरुषं पप्रच्छ ।
भगवन्नन्तर्लक्ष्यादिकं बहुधोक्तम् ।
मया तन्न ज्ञातम् ।
त्वद्ब्रूहि मह्यम् ॥१॥
तदा होवाच पञ्चभूतकारणं तडित्कूटाभं तद्वच्चतुःपीटम् ।
तन्मध्ये तत्त्वप्रकाशो भवति ।
सोऽतिगूढ अव्यक्तश्च ॥२॥
तज्ज्ञानप्लवाधिरूढेन ज्ञेयम् ।
तद्बाह्याभ्यन्तर्लक्ष्यम् ॥३॥

तन्मध्ये जगल्लीनम् ।
तन्नादबिन्दुकलातीतमखण्डमण्डलम् ।
तत्सगुणनिर्गुणस्वरूपम् ।
तद्वेत्ता विमुक्तः ।।४।।

आदावग्निमण्डलम् ।
तदुपरि सूर्यमण्डलम् ।
तन्मध्ये सुधाचन्द्रमण्डलम् ।
तन्मध्येऽखण्डब्रह्मतेजो मण्डलम् ।
तद्विद्युल्लेखावच्छुक्लभास्वरम् ।
तदेव शाम्भवीलक्षणम् ।।५।।

तद्दर्शने तिस्रो दृष्टयः अमा प्रतिपत् पूर्णिमा चेति ।
निमीलितदर्शनममादृष्टिः ।
अर्धोन्मीलितं प्रतिपत् ।
सर्वोन्मीलनं पूर्णिमा भवति ।
तासु पूर्णिमाभ्यासः कर्तव्यः ।।६।।
तल्लक्ष्यं नासाग्रम् ।
यदा तालुमूले गाढतमो दृश्यते ।
तदभ्यासादखण्डमण्डलाकारज्योतिर्दृश्यते ।
तदेव सच्चिदानन्दं ब्रह्म भवति ।।७।।

एवं सहजानन्दे यदा मनो लीयते तदा शाम्भवी भवति ।
तामेव खेचरीमाहुः ।।८।।
तदभ्यासान्मनःस्थैर्यम्

ततो बुद्धिस्थैर्यम् ।।९।।
तच्चिह्नानि आदौ तारकवद्दृश्यते ।
ततो वह्रदर्पणम् ।
तत उपरि पूर्णचन्द्रमण्डलम् ।
ततो नवरत्न प्रभामण्डलम् ।
ततो मध्याह्नार्कमण्डलम् ।
ततो वह्निशिखामण्डलं क्रमाद्दृश्यते ।।१०।।

द्वितीयः खण्डः

तदा पश्चिमाभिमुखप्रकाशः
स्फटिकधूम्रबिन्दुनादकलानक्षत्रखद्योतदीपनेत्रसुवर्णनवरत्नादिप्र
भा
दृश्यन्ते ।
तदेव प्रणवस्वरूपम् ।।१।।
प्राणापानयोरैक्यं कृत्वा धृतकुम्भको
नासाग्रदर्शनदृढभावनया द्विकराङ्गुलिभिः
षण्मुखीकरणेन प्रणवध्वनिं निशम्य मनस्तत्र लीनं भवति
।।२।।
तस्य न कर्मलेपः ।
रवेरुदयास्तमययोः किल कर्म कर्तव्यम् ।
एवंविधश्चिदादीत्यस्योदयास्तमयाभावात्सर्वकर्माभावः ।।३।।
शब्दकाललयेन दिवारात्र्यतीतो भूत्वा
सर्वपरिपूर्णज्ञानेनोन्मन्यवस्थावशेन ब्रमैक्यं भवति ।
उन्मन्या अमनस्कं भवति ।।४।।

तस्य निश्चिन्ता ध्यानम् । सर्वकर्मनिराकरणमावाहनम् ।
निश्चयज्ञमासनम् । उन्मनीभावः पाद्यम् ।
सदाऽमनस्कमर्घ्यम् । सदादीप्तिरपारामृतवृत्तिः स्नानम् ।
सर्वत्र भावना गन्धः । दृक॑स्वरूपावस्थानमक्षताः ।
चिदाप्तिः पुष्पम् । चिदग्निस्वरूपं दूपः ।
चिदादित्यस्वरूपं दीपः ।
परिपूर्णचन्द्रामृतरसस्यैकीकरणं नैवेद्यम् ।
निश्चलत्वं प्रदक्षिणम् । सोऽहंभावो नमस्कारः ।
मौनं स्तुतिः । सर्वसंतोषो विसर्जनमिति य एवं वेद ।।५।।

तृतीयः खण्डः

एवं त्रिपुट्यां निरस्तायां निस्तरङ्गसमुद्रवन्निवातस्थितदीपवद-
चलसंपूर्णभावाभावविहीनकैवल्यज्योतिर्भवति ।।१।।
जाग्रन्निद्रान्तः परिज्ञानेन ब्रह्मविद्भवति ।।२।।

सुषुप्तिसमाध्योर्मनोलयाविशेषोऽपि
महदस्त्युभयोर्भेदस्तमसि लीनत्वान्मुक्तिहेतुत्वाभावाच्च ।।३।।
समाधौ मृदिततमोविकारस्य
तदाकाराकारिताखण्डाकारवृत्त्यात्मकसाक्षिचैतन्ये
प्रपञ्चलयः संपद्यते प्रपञ्चस्य मनः कल्पितत्वात् ।।४।।
ततो भेदाभावात् कदाचिद्बहिर्गतेऽपि मिथ्यात्वभानात् ।
सकृद्विभातसदानन्दानुभवैकगोचरो ब्रह्मवित्तदैव भवात ।।५।।

ततो भेदाभावात् कदाचिद्बहिर्गतेऽपि मिथ्यात्वभानात् ।
दकृद्विभातसदानन्दानुभवैकगोचरो ब्रह्मवित्तदैव भवति ।।५।।
तस्य संकल्पनाशः स्यात्तस्य मुक्तिः करे स्थिता ।
तस्माद्भावाभावौ परित्यज्य परमात्मध्यानेन मुक्तो भवति
।।६।।
पुनःपुनः सर्वावस्थासु ज्ञानज्ञेयौ ध्यानध्येयौ लक्ष्यालक्ष्ये
दृश्यादृश्ये चोहापोहादि परित्यज्य जीवन्मुक्तो भवेत् ।
य एवं वेद ।।७।।

चतुर्थः खण्डः

पञ्चावस्थाः जाग्रत्स्वप्नसुषुप्तितुरीयतुरीयातीताः ।।१।।
जाग्रति प्रवृत्तो जीवः प्रवृत्तिमार्गासक्तः ।
पापफलनरकादि मास्तु शुभकर्मफलस्वर्गमस्त्विति कङ्क्षते
।।२।।
एवं स एव स्वीकृतवैराग्यात्कर्मफलजन्माऽलं ।
संसारबन्धनमलमिति विमुक्त्यभिमुखो निवृत्तिमार्गप्रवृत्तो भवति
।।३।।

स एव संसारणाय गुरुमाश्रित्य कामादि त्यक्त्वा
विहितकर्मचरन्साधनचतुष्टयसंपन्नो हृदयकमलमध्ये
भगवत्सत्तामात्रान्तर्लक्ष्यरूपमासाद्य सुषुप्त्यवस्थाया
मुक्तब्रह्मानन्दस्मृतिं लब्ध्वा एक एवाहमद्वितीयः
कंचित्कालमज्ञानवृत्त्या तदुभयनिवृत्त्या प्राज्ञ
इदानीमस्मीत्यहमेक एव स्थानभेदादावस्थाभेदस्य

परंतु नहि मदन्यदिति जातविवेकः शुद्धाद्वैतब्रह्माहमिति भिदागन्धं निरस्य स्वान्तर्विजृम्भितभानुमण्डलध्यानतदाकाराकारितपरंब्रह्माकारितमुक्तिमार्गमारूढः परिपक्वो भवाति ।।४।।

संकल्पादिकं मनो बन्धहेतुः ।
तद्युक्तं मनो मोक्षाय भवति ।।५।।
तद्वांश्चक्षुरादिबाह्यप्रपञ्चोपरतो विगतप्रपञ्चगन्धः सर्वजगदात्मत्वेन पश्यंस्त्यक्ताहंकारो ब्रह्माहमस्मीति चिन्तयन्निदं सर्वं यदयमात्मेति भावयन्कृत्यो भवति ।।६।।

पञ्चमः खण्डः

सर्वपरिपूर्णतुरीयातीतब्रह्मभूतो योगी भवति ।
तं ब्रह्मेति स्तुवन्ति ।।१।।
सर्वलोकस्तुतिपात्रः सर्वदेशसंचारशीलः परमात्मगगने बिन्दुं निक्षिप्य शुद्धाद्वैताजाड्यसहजामनस्कयोगनिद्राखण्डानन्दपदानुवृत्त्या भवाति ।।२।।
तच्चानन्दसमुद्रमग्ना योगिनो भवन्ति ।।३।।
तदपेक्षया इन्द्रादयः स्वल्पानन्दाह ।
एवं प्राप्तानन्दः परमयोगी भवतीत्युपनिषत् ।।४।।

तृतीयं ब्राह्मणम्

प्रथमः खण्डः

याज्ञवल्क्यो महामुनिर्मण्डलपुरुषं पप्रच्छ
स्वामिन्नमनस्कलक्षणमुक्तमपि विस्मृतं
पुनस्तल्लक्षणं ब्रूहीति ।।१।।
तथेति मण्डलपुरुषोऽब्रवीत् ।
इदममनस्कमतिरहस्यम् ।
यज्ज्ञानेन कृतार्थो भवति तन्नित्यं शांभवीमुद्रान्वितं ।।२।।

परमात्मदृष्टया तत्प्रत्ययलक्ष्याणि दृष्ट्वा तदनु
सर्वेशमप्रमेयमजं शिवं परमाकाशं निरालम्बमद्वयं
ब्रह्मविष्णुरुद्रादीनामेकलक्ष्यं सर्वकारणं परंब्रह्मात्मन्येव
पश्यमानो गुहाविहरणमेव निश्चयेन ज्ञात्वा
भावाभावादिद्वन्दवातीतः
संविदितमनोन्मन्यनुभवस्तदनन्तरमखिलेन्द्रियक्षयवशादमनस्क
-सुखब्रह्मानन्दसमुद्रेमनः प्रवाहयोगरूपनिवातस्थितदीपवदचलं
परंब्रह्म प्राप्नोति ।।३।।

ततः शुष्कवृष्कवन्मुर्र्छानिद्रामय
निःश्वासोच्छ्वासाभावान्नष्टद्वन्द्वः
सदाऽचञ्चलगात्रः परमशान्तिं स्वीकृत्य मनःप्रचारशून्यं
परमात्मनि लीनं भवति ।।४।।
पयःस्नावानन्तरं धेनुस्तनक्षीरमिव सर्वेन्द्रियवर्गे
परिनष्टे मनोनाशो भवति तदेवामनस्कम् ।।५।।
तदनु नित्यशुद्धः परमात्माहमेवेति तत्त्वमसीत्युपदेशेन
त्वमेवाहमहमेव त्वमिति तारकयोगमार्गेणाखण्डानन्दपूर्णः

कृतार्थो भवति ।।६।।

द्वितीयः खण्डः

परिपूर्णपराकाशमग्नमनः प्राप्तोन्मन्यवस्थः
संन्यस्तसर्वेन्द्रियवर्गोऽनेकजन्मार्जितपुण्यपुञ्ज-
पक्वकैवल्यफलोऽखण्डानन्दनिरस्तसर्वक्लेशमलो
ब्रह्माहमस्मीति कृतकृत्यो भवति ।।१।।
त्वमेवाहं न भेदोऽस्ति पूर्णत्वात्परमात्मनः ।
इत्युच्चरन्त्समालिङ्ग्य शिष्यं ज्ञप्तिमनीनयत् ।।२।।

चतुर्थं ब्राह्मणम

अथ ह याज्ञवल्क्यो मण्डलपुरुषं पप्रच्छ
व्योमपञ्चकलक्षणं विस्तरेणानुब्रूहीति ।।१।।
स होवाचाकाशं पराकाशं महाकाशं ।
सूर्याकाशं परमाकाशमिति पञ्च भवन्ति ।।२।।
बाह्याभ्यन्तरमन्धकारमयमाकाशम् ।
बाह्यस्याभ्यन्तरे कालानलसदृशं पराकाशम् ।
सबाह्याभ्यन्तरेऽपरिमितद्युतिनिभं तत्त्वं महाकाशम् ।
सबाह्याभ्यन्तरे सूर्यनिभं सूर्याकाशम् ।
अनिर्वचनीयज्योतिः सर्वव्यापकं निरतिशयानन्दलक्षणं
परमाकाशम् ।।३।।
एवं तत्त्वल्लक्ष्यदर्शनात्तत्तद्रूपो भवति ।।४।।
नवचक्रं षडाधारं त्रिलक्ष्यं व्योमपञ्चकम् ।

सम्यगेतन्न जानाति स योगी नामतो भवेत् ।।५।।

पञ्चमं ब्राह्मणम

सविषयं मनो बन्धाय निर्विषयं मुक्तये भवति ।।१।।
अतः सर्वं जगच्चित्तगोचरम् ।
तदेव चित्तं निराश्रयं मनोन्मन्यवस्थापरिपत्नं
लययोग्यं भवति ।।२।।
तल्लयं परिपूर्णे मयि समभ्यसेत्
मनोलयकारणमहमेव ।।३।।

अनाहतस्य शब्दस्य तस्य शब्दस्य यो ध्वनिः ।
ध्वनेरन्तर्गतं ज्योतिर्ज्योतिरन्तर्गतं मनः ।।४।।
यन्मनस्त्रिजगत्सृष्टिस्थितिव्यसनकर्मकृत् ।
तन्मनो विलयं याति तद्विष्णो परमं पदम् ।।५।।

तल्लयाच्छुद्धाद्वैतसिद्धिर्भेदाभावात् ।
एतदेव परमतत्त्वम् ।।६।।
स तज्ज्ञो बालोन्मत्तपिशाचवज्जडवृत्त्या लोकमाचरेत् ।।७।।
एवममनस्काभ्यासेनैवनित्यतृपतिरल्पमूत्रपुरीषमित
भोजनदृढाङ्गाजाड्यनिद्रादृग्वायुचलनाभावब्रह्म-
दर्शनाज्ज्ञातसुखस्वरूपसिद्धिर्भवति ।।८।।

एवं चिरसमाधिजनितब्रह्मामृतपानपरायणोऽसै
संन्यासी परमहंस अवधूतो भवति ।

तद्दर्शनेन सकलं जगत्पवित्रं भवति ।
तत्सेवापरोऽपि मुक्तो भवति ।
तत्कुलमेकोत्तरशतं तारयति ।
तन्मातृपितृजायापत्यवर्गं च मुक्तं भवतीत्पनिषत् ।।९।।

इत्युपनिषत्

E. Continuous Translation

Advaya-Tāraka-Upaniṣad

Opening Invocation
Om, that is full, this is full. From the full comes the full.
If the full is taken from the full, only the full remains.

1.
Now we have an exposition of the *advaya-tāraka-upaniṣad* for the sage [and] ascetic [who is] filled [with] the six qualities of equanimity, self-control etc.

2 to 4.
Always recognising 'I am the nature of Consciousness', [with] eyes completely shut or eyes somewhat open, by looking inward slightly above the eyebrows, [then] beholding the Supreme Reality, [in] the form of a multitude [of] fires [of] Being-Consciousness-Bliss, one becomes that form.

Thus [the yogin] can save himself from the great fear of the cycle of conception, birth, old age [and] death. This is Tāraka. Having discerned the illusory individual and transcendental [and] abandoned all differentiation, saying 'not this, not that', that which remains is the nondual Absolute.

5.
[There] exists in the middle of the body the *brahmanāḍī* [within] *suṣumnā*, of the form of the sun [and] the lustre of the full moon. Arising from the root cakra, it extends to the *brahmarandhra*, the opening at the crown of the head. In its centre is the renowned *kuṇḍalinī*, with a radiance equal to a crore of lightning flashes [and] subtle [of] limb like the thread [of] the fibrous lotus root. Having seen it through the mind alone, a person becomes liberated through the destruction of all sin. If he incessantly sees with eyes wide

open the radiance of *tāraka-yoga* leaping forth in a specific area from the forehead, he is an adept. Then the blowing sound *phū* is produced in the two ear orifices, blocked with the tips of the forefingers. Then, beholding in [that] firm state of mind [that] place [as] a blue light gone to the middle of the eyes, he attains, by looking inward, unequalled bliss. He realises thus in the heart. Such [is] the perception [of] the inner sign by those wishing for liberation.

6.
Now the external sign [is described]. If he sees [at a distance from] the nosetip of four, six, eight, ten [and] twelve digit-lengths respectively a space doubly endowed with a bright yellow colour, a quivering wave [of] red-like glistening [and] dark blue, then he is a yogin. There are rays of light in the foremost range of vision of the person scanning with wandering vision the space. By seeing that, he becomes a yogin.

[When] he sees rays of light sparkling like molten gold at the outer corners of the eyes or on the ground, that vision is fixed. [Whoever] sees twelve digit-lengths above the head attains immortality. If [he has] the vision [of] the lustre of space in the head, wherever he is, is indeed a yogin.

7 and 8.
Now the intermediate sign [is described]. [The yogin] sees various coloured images in the early morning like the whole orb of the sun [or] like a row of flames of fire [or] like the regions between heaven and earth without these. Having the shape of this form, he abides there. By seeing this again [and again] he becomes the space devoid of qualities. He becomes the supreme space resembling the unfathomable darkness radiant with the dazzling form of *tāraka*. He becomes the great space like the illumination of the fire of time. He becomes the elemental space, radiant with supreme lustre, superior [to] all. He becomes the solar space, [having the]

appearance [of] the dazzling glory of a hundred thousand suns. Thus the fivefold space, external and internal is the sign of tāraka, the deliverer. [Whoever] experiences this, freed from the fruit, becomes like such space. Thus only the sign of tāraka is the bestower [of] the fruit [of] *amanaska*, mindlessness.

That tāraka [is] twofold: the earlier half is tāraka and the latter half mindlessness. There is a verse about this saying: 'That yoga [is] the twofold way, made of the earlier and the latter. The earlier is known as tāraka, and the latter mindlessness'.

9.

In the pupils in the interior of the eyes, there is the reflection of the sun and moon. Seeing the sun and moon discs through the pupils is like [seeing] the macrocosm as the microcosm in the space in the centre of the head, having ascertained it is the double point on the disc. One should contemplate with fixed mind, through the perception [of] looking upon the two as one, looking there for some time through the pupils, [as] without this connection, [there is] no scope for the way of the senses. Thus tāraka should be investigated through introspection only.

10.

That tāraka is twofold: tāraka with form and tāraka without form. That which stops with the senses [is] with form. That which transcends the pair of eyebrows [is] without form. In every case in examining the inner object, constant practice with a fixed mind is necessary. Through the pupils [and] the pure vision [of] that which dwells beyond, through introspection and a steady mind, [the yogin experiences] Being-Consciousness-Bliss as the essential nature [of] Brahman. Hence Brahman, consisting of white radiance, is clear. That Brahman becomes known by the eye, assisted by the mind in introspection. Thus also the formless tāraka [is known]. Through the fixed mind, through the eye alone, the minuscule and others become known. Because of the dependence of mind and eye for the purpose of perception of form, external and internal, [it is] only through the combination of the eye, mind and Self [that] the action of perception of form can succeed. Thus inner vision [with] a fixed mind becomes the light of tāraka.

11.

By means of the sight [being fixed] on the cavern [in] the centre of the pair of eyebrows, the radiance dwelling above becomes visible. [This is] tāraka yoga. Through this, having united with careful effort tāraka [and] the fixed mind, [the yogin] should raise the pair of eyebrows somewhat. This is the former part of tāraka yoga. The latter, however, is without form [and] is said [to be] beyond the mind. There exists a great ray of light in the part above the root of the palate. It should be meditated on by the yogins. From that comes the power [of] *aṇima* and others.

12.

If there is the vision of the inner and outer sign, [at the same time] devoid [of the power] of opening and closing the eyes, this is the true *śāṃbhavī mudrā*. Because of the sojourn of sages [who have] ascended to this mudrā, the earth becomes purified. Having seen this, all worlds are purified. He who is permitted homage to such great yogins is also liberated.

13.

The radiant light [of] the inner sign is the essential form of the nondual Reality. Through instruction by a superior spiritual teacher, the inner sign becomes the radiant light at the thousand-petalled [lotus] or the light hidden in the cavern of the *buddhi*, or the fourth consciousness abiding at the end of the sixteenth. The sight of that [is] dependent on a true teacher.

14 to 18.

A spiritual teacher [is] conversant in the *vedas*, a devotee of Viṣṇu, free from jealousy, intent on yoga, [has] the wisdom of yoga, and always [in] the pure nature of yoga. [He who is] endowed with devotion to the teacher [and who is] especially a knower of the Self, thus possessed with [these] qualities is deemed a spiritual teacher. Now the sound *gu* is darkness. The sound *ru* is its obstruction. Because of the obstruction of darkness, he is named a *guru*. The guru alone [is] the Supreme Reality. The guru alone [is] the supreme way. The guru alone [is] supreme knowledge. The guru alone [is] the supreme refuge. The guru alone [is] the supreme aim. The guru alone [is] supreme wealth. Because he [is] the teacher of that, therefore the guru is greater.

19.

Whoever causes [this] to be uttered once becomes liberated from mundane existence. At that very moment the sin committed [in] every birth disappears. He gains all desires. He has fulfilment of all human goals. Whoever knows this [knows] the upaniṣad.

Thus concludes the Advaya-Tāraka-Upaniṣad.

Maṇḍalabrāhmaṇa Upaniṣad

Opening Invocation

Remember Rāmacandra, the one accomplished [in] *rāja yoga*, the expansion of the five subtle spaces, the form of *tāraka* within Brāhman.
That [is] full. Om is divine peace.

First Brāhmaṇa

First Section

1.
The great sage Yājñavalkya went to the world of the Sun. Bowing to the Sun, he said to Him: 'o blessed Lord Āditya, describe [to me] the essence of the soul'.

2 and 3.
He, Nārāyaṇa, replied thus: it is said [to be] the eightfold [path of] yoga beginning with *yama* [and] combined with *jñāna*. The conquest of cold and heat, food and sleep, constant unchangeable peace and the restraint [of] the sense organs, these [are] the yamas.

4 and 5.
The *niyamas* [are] devotion to *guru*, dedication to the path of truth, enjoyment of things [which] come from joy, and through the enjoyment of these things, contentment, detachment, a secluded abode, cessation of thought and an attitude of detachment [from] the craving for the fruits [of actions]. An āsana [which is] a comfortable posture [with] a [steady] mind for a long time is indeed a niyama.

6 to 11.
Prāṇāyāma [is] through inhalation, breath retention and exhalation, with the count of sixteen, sixty-four and thirty-two [*mātrās*] respectively. *Pratyāhāra* [is] the restraining of

the mind from the objects of the senses. *Dhāraṇa* is drawing the mind away from objects [of the senses and] fixing [it] on consciousness. *Dhyāna* [is] the attention fixed on the one consciousness in all bodies. *Samādhi* is the forgetting [of the individual self] in *dhyāna*. These are the subtle limbs [of yoga]. Whoever knows this, he attains liberation.

Second Section

1 to 3.
There are five faults in the body: sensual desire, anger, incorrect breathing, fear [and] sleep. The removal of these [can be achieved by] reverence for the *tattvas*, caution, a light diet, forbearance [and] lack of desires. To cross the ocean of *saṃsāra* [which is] the serpent of sleep and fear, the wave of violence etc, the whirlpool of greed, the mire of a wife, adhering to the subtle paths [and] without transgressing the quality of *sattva* etc, one should observe *Tāraka*.

4 to 6.
Tāraka, the deliverer [with] the form of the unchanging spirit of *sat-cit-ānanda* [of] Brahman [is] at the eyebrow centre. Seeing through the three points of concentration [is] the way to it. *Suṣumnā*, [which goes] from *mūlādhāra* up to *brahmarandhra* [is] as bright as the sun. In its centre [is] *kuṇḍalinī*, [bright] as crores of lightning [and] subtle [as] the fibrous root of a lotus. Destruction of *tamas* [is] there. Through insight into it, [there is] destruction of all sins.

7 to 12.
When the orifices of the two ears are closed by the tips of the forefingers, a sound of blowing is produced. When the mind is fixed there, it sees a blue light between the eyes, thus also in the heart. [When] one sees the external object at the nosetip, by four, six, eight, ten and twelve finger widths in succession, bright blue like the sky [then] like a dark-coloured garment, [then] quivering [like] a red wave, [and

then] the two colours yellow and orange together, one [is] a yogin.

[When,] moving the eyes, a person sees two parts of the sky, rays of light occur at the corner of the eyes. Then his vision becomes steady. [When] he sees a light of twelve finger widths above his head, then he goes to the immortal state. [When] the object [is] in the middle, he sees in the morning folds of various bright colours of the sun, moon, fire and water as if separate from the sky. Then he has their nature and appearance.

13 to 14.
Through practice he becomes the unchangeable *ākāśa* free from attributes. He becomes the supreme ākāśa [which] removes deep darkness [by] the appearance [of] the glittering star. He becomes the great ākāśa luminous like the fire of time. He becomes the elemental ākāśa, radiant, unique, supreme, the best of all. He becomes the solar ākāśa, appearing as bright as crores of suns. He who knows thus, through practice thus becomes absorbed in [them].

Third Section

1 to 6.
Know that yoga [is] twofold, [divided] equally into earlier and later. The earlier is known as *tāraka*; the later is called *amanaska*. Tāraka [is] of two kinds. There is tāraka with form and tāraka without form. That which ends with the senses is tāraka with form. That which [is] beyond both eyebrows is tāraka without form. One should also practise both through the mind. The inner vision through the mind reveals tāraka. The golden flame appears in the cavern between the two eyebrows. This [is] the earlier tāraka. And the later [is] amanaska. The great light is above the root of the palate. Through the sight of it [arise] *siddhis*, such as

making the body small. When the [spiritual] vision [is] internalised and the eyes [see] outward without blinking, this is *śāmbhavī mudrā*. [This] great knowledge is kept secret in all the *tantras*. Through this knowledge *saṃsāra* ceases. This practice gives the fruit of liberation. The inner object becomes fluid light. It is known by the great *ṛṣis* [and] cannot be seen through the internal and external senses.

Fourth Section

1 to 4.
The inner object [of concentration] at *sahasrāra* [is] fluid light. Others say the inner object [is] the form of *puruṣa* in the cave of the *buddhi*, beautiful [in] all his limbs. Some say the inner object [is] the auspicious blue-necked five-faced one, accompanied by Umā, [and which] goes to the centre of the sphere inside the head. Some say *puruṣa*, the size of a thumb, [is] the inner object. All [these], it is said, [are] the different perceptions of the one *ātman*. Whoever sees the meditation object from the viewpoint [of] the pure ātman, he indeed becomes firmly established in Brahman.

The *jīva*, consisting of twenty-five parts, having abandoned the self-made twenty-four *tattwas*, becomes a *jivanmukta* through the conviction [that] the twenty-sixth [tattwa] is 'I am *paramātmā*'. Thus, through the vision of the inner object of meditation, having become the object of meditation oneself, while in the liberated state, one becomes the indivisible sphere of the transcendent ether.

Second Brāhmaṇa

First Section

1 to 4.
Then Yājñavalkya did ask the *puruṣa* in the sphere of the sun: "O Lord, *antarlakṣya* has been described many times

before, [yet] it has not been understood by me. [Please] explain it for me." He did reply thus: "[It is] the cause of the five elements [and has] the lustre of many {flashes of] lightning, likewise its four seats. In the middle of that is the light of its essence, secret and subtle. This is to be known by embarking on the boat of wisdom. The object of meditation is [both] external and internal. In its midst the world is absorbed. It [is] the indivisible sphere beyond the potential for the manifestation of the inner sound. Its form [is] with and without attributes. [Whoever] knows this is liberated.

5.

At first the region of fire [is seen], above it the region of the sun, in its middle the region of the heavenly moon, [then] in its middle the region of the indivisible radiance of the *brahman*. It [is] resplendent like a streak [of] white lightning. That is the sign of *śāmbhavī*.

6 to 7.

Upon seeing it there are three views, *amā*, new moon, *pratipat*, first phase of the lunar fortnight, and *pūrṇimā* full moon. The sight of amā is looking with closed eyes, of pratipat with half-opened eyes, of pūrṇimā with fully-opened eyes. Of these the practice of pūrṇimā should be done. Its focus [is] the nosetip, when a deep darkness is seen at the root of the palate. Through this practice a light [of] the form [of] an indivisible sphere is seen. This alone is Brahman, *sat-cit-ānanda*.

8 to 10.

When the mind is absorbed in its innate bliss, then *śambhavī* appears. That alone is called the *khecarī*. Through its practice [there is] firmness [of] the mind, then firmness of the intellect. [Here are] its signs: first it is seen like a star; then a diamond, a mirror; then the disc of the full moon above; then a crown of rays [with] nine gems; then the sphere of the midday sun; then a circle of flames is seen in its turn.

Second Section

1 to 4.
Then [comes] the light directed towards the west [where] the glow of crystal, smoke, *bindu*, inner sound, *kalā*, star, firefly, lamp, eye, gold, nine gems etc are seen. This alone is the true form of *praṇava.*

Having united *prāṇa* and *apāna* [and] maintained breath retention, with strong willpower concentrated on the nosetip, [and] by performing *ṣaṇmukhī* with the two forefingers, hearing the sound of praṇava, the mind becomes absorbed there. This person is not tainted with *karma*. The karma [of rituals] is indeed to be done at the rising and setting of the sun. Thus [for] the one who knows [that] the rising and setting of the sun [of] pure consciousness [comes] from the heart, [there is] absence [of] all karma.

Having become [one who has gone] beyond day and night through the dissolution of sound and time, he becomes one with Brahman through the power [of] the state beyond mind, all-perfect wisdom. Through mindlessness there is freedom from thought.

5.
When there is firmness [of mind], [there is] *dhyānam*. The removal [of] all actions [is] an invocation. [It is] abiding in wisdom through conviction. The state of mindlessness [is necessary for] *pādya*. *Arghya* [is done] always [when] the mind is free from thought. The state [of] eternal light [and] unlimited nectar [is] *snāna*. The application [of] *gandha* [is] everywhere. Abiding in one's true form [through] the spiritual eye [is] *akṣata*. Attaining pure consciousness [is worshipped with] flower. Incense [is] the essential form of the fire of consciousness. The lamp's light [is] the essential form of the sun of consciousness. Uniting with the nectar [of] the full moon [is] *naivedya*. Motionless [is]

circumambulation. The attitude 'I am That' [is] offering reverence. Silence [is] praise. Contentment in all concludes [worship]. So says whoever knows this.

Third Section

1 and 2.
When the *tripuṭī* are thus removed, one becomes the light of final liberation free from existence and non-existence, whole, immobile, like a calm ocean, [as] still as a lamp in a windless [place]. One becomes a knower of Brahman through awareness of the waking state to the end of sleep.

3 and 4.
The main similarity between deep sleep and *samādhi* is the loss of consciousness in both, and the difference [is] the absence [of] the cause of liberation [as it is] concealed in *tamas*. In samādhi, when the crushed tamas is transformed, then the form of the mind takes the shape of the formless, having the nature of the consciousness of the witness, [in which] the dissolution of the universe is absorbed, the mind presumed to exist as the manifestation of the whole world.

5 and 7.
Therefore, even though [one has] sometimes externalised because of the absence of difference [and] false perception, the knower of Brahman is indeed the [one who] attains the unique experience of true bliss [which] dawned spontaneously. Liberation is firmly in the hand of one whose volition is destroyed. Having thus abandoned [ideas of] existence and non-existence, one is liberated by meditating on the Supreme Spirit.

Having relinquished again and again in all the states [of consciousness] knowledge and what is to be known, meditation and what is to be meditated on, the target and lack of target, the visible and invisible, and reasoning and argument and so forth, one becomes a *jīvanmukta*. Whoever knows thus [becomes a *jīvanmukta*].

Fourth Section

1 to 3.

The five states [of consciousness are] waking, dreaming, deep sleep, *turīya* and beyond *turīya*. The *jīva* [who is] engaged in the waking state [and] attached to the worldly path longs for [this], saying: 'let [me] not have the fruit of [my] wrongdoings in hell etc, let me have the fruit of my auspicious actions [in] heaven'.

This very same person, having taken an aversion [to mundane life], saying 'enough [of] rebirths [due to] the fruits of [my] actions, enough of bondage to the cycle of birth, death and rebirth,' becomes committed to the path of introversion, approaching final emancipation.

4.

Thus he, having recourse to a spiritual teacher [in order to be liberated] from the mundane world, giving up all sensory pleasures, engaged in prescribed actions, endowed with the four *sādhanas*, attaining, in the centre of the lotus of the heart the reality [of] the inner vision [which is] the form [of] the Lord, evoking the memory [of] the bliss [of] the liberated brahman [experienced] in the state [of] deep sleep, 'I am one without a second. Because of the condition [of] ignorance for some time [and] as a consequence of forgetting the impressions [in my] waking state, I am [in] the dreaming state. Having left both [states] I am now only the one *prājña*. There is nothing else beyond me [although] I have different states due to the difference [in] place. Having cast out the scent of distinction I, [who have] innate discrimination, [am] the pure non-dual Brahman.'

Having attained the path of liberation, [which is] the nature of the transcendent Brahman, [after] assuming its form and appearance by meditating on the sphere of the sun manifested within himself, he becomes ripe [for emancipation].

5 to 6.

The mind, [with] its volition and so on, [is] the cause [of] bondage. The mind freed of these has liberation. Thus, free from the external visible world of sight and other [senses], away from its odour, seeing all worlds through the essence of the *ātman*, having renounced the individual self, knowing 'I am Brahman', considering all this [as] this ātman, becoming one who has done his duty, he becomes [liberated].

Fifth Section

1 to 4.

The yogin is [one who] has become the all-complete transcendent Brahman. [People] worship him as Brahman. This virtuous one [becomes] a vessel [of] praise [in] the whole world, wandering through all countries, having cast his *bindu* into the ether [of] the Supreme Consciousness, following the path of the uninterrupted bliss of *yoga-nidrā* [produced by] the pure non-dual vital innate thoughtless state, he becomes [one with Brahman].

And then the yogin becomes immersed in the ocean of bliss. Compared with this, the bliss of Indra and others is minute. Thus having attained this bliss, he becomes the Supreme Yogin. So says the *upaniṣad.*

Third Brāhmaṇa
First Section

1 and 2.

The great sage Yājñavalkya asked the *puruṣa* of the sphere [of the sun]: 'o Master, although I have been told the meaning of amanaska, [I have] forgotten [it]. Please explain its meaning again'.

Thus the puruṣa of the sphere [of the sun] said: 'this amanaska is a profound mystery. By knowing this, one becomes [a person who] has fulfilled one's duties. This is always connected with *śāṃbhavī-mudrā'*.

3.
By contemplating the *paramātman* [and] seeing [that] thereupon [as] the aim of meditation whole, unborn, immeasurable, auspicious, the transcendent ether, independent, non-dual the one goal [of] Brahma, Viṣṇu, Rudra and others, seeing in the one *ātman* the Supreme Reality, the cause of all, without doubt knowing the roaming in the cave [of the heart], free from the opposites of existence and non-existence and others, understanding the experience [of] *unmani* of the mind, then by living without all the senses, one attains the Supreme Reality [which is] motionless like a lamp [in] a windless place, [taking] the form [of] merging with the river of the mind with the ocean of the bliss of Brahman [and] the delight in the mindless state.

4 to 6.
Then, like a dried-up tree, the dual [state] consisting of lethargy and sleep, lost through the absence of exhalation and inhalation, the body always steady, having acquired absolute peace, the mind empty [of] activity, one becomes dissolved in the Supreme Spirit. The destruction of the mind is when all groups of the senses are destroyed like the milk in the cow's udder after the glands [are emptied of] milk. Only that is mindlessness.

Thereupon, having done one's duty, one becomes ever pure, [and] through the path of *tāraka yoga*, full [of] undivided bliss, thinking 'I am the Supreme Spirit alone', implying 'You are That', 'You are I alone', 'I am You alone'.

Second Section

1 and 2.

The state of *unmani* having been attained, the mind immersed in the fullness of the Supreme Space, the group of all the senses relinquished, [and] all sorrows and impurities dispelled, [now] in undivided bliss, the fruit [of] a myriad of merits [from] various previous births ripened [into] emancipation, thinking 'I am Brahman', [the yogin] becomes one who has fulfilled his duty.

'I am you alone.' There is no difference due to the fullness of the Supreme Self. Saying thus, dearly embracing his disciple [Yajñavalkya], he [the puruṣa] brought [him] to this understanding.

Fourth Brāhmaṇa

1 to 5.

Hence Yājñavalkya asked the Lord of the Sphere [of the Sun]: 'please explain in detail the fivefold kinds [of] ether'. He replied thus: 'there are five [kinds of ether]: *ākāśa, parākāśa, mahākāśa, sūryākāśa* and *paramākāśa*.

Ākāśa consists of outer and inner darkness. Pārākāśa [is] like the fire of all-destroying time, [both] outer and inner. The essence of mahākāśa [is] like unlimited brilliance, [both] outer and inner. Sūryākāśa resembles the outer and inner sun. Paramākāśa [is] the light beyond description, all-pervading [and of] the nature of ultimate bliss. Thus by concentration on its nature, one becomes that form.

Whoever does not have the correct knowledge of the nine *cakras*, six *ādhāras*, three *lakṣyas* [and] five *ākāśas* is a yogin in name [only].

Fifth Brāhmaṇa

1 to 3.

The thinking mind attached to sensual objects is in bondage, [whereas the mind] not attached to sensual objects becomes liberated. Thus all the world [is in] the domain of *citta*, the storehouse of the mind. That citta, independent, fully ripened into the *unmani* state of the mind, becomes dissolved into union [with Brahman]. One should practise this dissolution in me [who am] completely full. I alone am the cause [of] the dissolution of the mind.

4 and 5.

When a sound [arises from] the heart, [there is] an echo of that sound, light penetrating the echo, the mind penetrating the light, which mind is the maker of creation, preservation [and] destruction of the three worlds. That mind becomes dissolved in the supreme seat of Viṣṇu.

6 to 8.

Through this dissolution [there is] the perfection of the pure non-dual state, due to the absence of division. This alone [is] the highest truth. He who knows this behaves in the world like a demon, madman [or] child in the manner [of] an idiot.

Thus through the practice of amanaska alone, ever content, [having] little urine and faeces [and] less food, strong in body, without sluggishness or sleep, eyes and vital airs without movement, having realised a vision of Brahman, he attains the nature of bliss.

9.

Thus the yogin, wholly intent on drinking the nectar of the Brahman produced by long [states of] transcendental awareness, becomes a *paramahaṃsa* [and] *avadhūta.* By seeing this the whole world becomes purified. Even an ignorant person intent on service to that becomes liberated. He causes one hundred and one [generations of his] family to cross to the north, and the whole [family], mother, father, wife, progeny becomes liberated.

Thus [ends] the upanişad.

F. Swami Satyadharma

On 12th June 2019 on the Central Coast of New South Wales Australia, our beloved Swami Satyadharma left her body. It was the day of Ganga Dussehra, celebrating the descent to Earth of the goddess Ganga, Ganga the mother who gives nourishment to all her children.

Dedication in her commentaries on the Yoga Upanishads have been to all spiritual aspirants. Swami Satyadharma's life was dedicated for over forty years to providing spiritual nourishment and bringing the light of yoga to all those who attended her programs throughout the world.

Swami Satyadharma was born in 1946 to a middle-class family in Connecticut, USA. She was the youngest of three and lived surrounded by nature and animals. She recognised the spiritual energy of nature, and was never attracted to big cities.

In search of purpose and spiritual guidance she travelled for years throughout Europe, Africa and Asia, where she met many enlightened masters. She spent two years in Nepal studying with Tibetan Buddhists lamas. She was an accomplished musician of the flute and guitar, and spent two years at the University of Bengal studying the sitar. In Java, Indonesia, she first studied batik, and then took part in a meditation program in one of the Javanese mystical schools. Her teacher was a mahasiddha who was 'breathtaking, awe-inspiring and transformative'. He specifically singled her out and said 'you have a future if you study earnestly, and after a long time you will attain an elevated consciousness as a yoga teacher, and you'll spend the later part of your life travelling internationally, and you'll teach the highest-level yoga teachings'. She was directed by the master to go to Mungher, Bihar, India, where she would meet a great teacher, Swami

Satyananda, a disciple of Swami Sivananda. There she stayed for thirty-five years.

At the age of 28, she was initiated by Swami Satyananda into *pūrṇa sannyasa* (full renunciation), a Dashnami order connected with the Advaita Vedanta tradition established by Adi Shankaracharya to protect, preserve and propagate spiritual knowledge. She absorbed the teachings and worked hard for the ashram for the first twenty years she spent there.

Then she edited books written by Swami Satyananda and, under his guidance, travelled the world teaching a range of spiritual courses on the Yogic Scriptures. And teach she did in Australia, USA, Canada, India, Nepal, Tibet, China, Japan, Korea, Columbia, Greece, Germany, Hungary, Bulgaria, France, Italy, Indonesia, New Zealand. In all those countries she was invited to come back time and time again. She had a great ability to teach. Her vast knowledge of the ancient scriptures was amazing. It just flowed from her. When she taught it was like she stepped into another zone, where she spoke with profound insight. That is why, if Swami Satyadharma was running a course, people would sign up regardless of the topic. Her deep understanding of yoga was reflected in the numerous topics she taught.

Her later years were devoted to writing commentaries on the Yoga Upanishads. At the end of her life she had completed her commentary on Nādabindu, and had written her commentary on only nine verses of Dhyānabindu. No-one else has completed this commentary, or been asked to do so, as her commentaries were original and unique.

Swami Satyadharma's Programs, Retreats and Lectures

Programs
Awakening Kundalini, Meditations from the Tantras, Dancing with the Divine, Atma Darshan, Intuition, Guru

Tattwa, Shiva Sutras, Mantra Yantra and Mandala, Ashram Life, Sadhana, Chakra Meditation, Spiritual Life.

***Deepening Sadhana* Retreats**
Kriya Yoga, Tattwa Shuddhi, Chakra Shuddhi, Prana Vidya and Mahavidya Sadhana.

Lectures
During the years she lived in Australia, she gave many satsangs and lectures to students enrolled in Yogic Studies courses. Topics included Origins of Yoga, Samkhya Tantra Vedanta, Yoga Sutras, Koshas, Chakras, Gunas, Bhagavad Gita, SWAN Theory, Raja Yoga, Gyan Yoga, Bhakti Yoga, Karma Yoga, Hatha Yoga, Upanishads, Pranava, Shiva Shakti, Mantra & Nada, Mantra Yoga Nada Yoga, Mudra Bandha, Shatkarmas, Kundalini Yoga, Swara Yoga, Prana Pranayama, Pratyahara, Theory & Practice of Antar Mouna, Yoga Psychology, Yoga Philosophy, Yoga in India, Yoga Ecology, Yoga History, Path of the Rishis, Yamas Niyamas, Yoga & Religion, Meditation, Yoga Nidra, Addiction, Purpose in Life, Grief, Body-Mind Therapy, Opening the Heart, Perception, Models of Mind, Mind & Consciousness, Mind Management and Living Consciously.

I was privileged to have worked with Swami Satyadharma for nine years. Her unlimited love and teachings will live on well into the future.

Om Tat Sat
Srimukti

G. Author's Note

I started working with Swami Satyadharma early in 2010, collating teachings on Bhakti Yoga, Rāja Yoga and Jñāna Yoga. I then had a yoga studio is Sydney, Australia, where I would invite senior teachers to give weekend programs. Swami Satyadharma had agreed to give a program on *Prāṇa Prāṇāyama Prāṇa Vidyā.* As usual with her programs, it was booked out well in advance. In 2011 she gave a program on *Managing the Mind through Meditation* and in 2014 *Yoga of the Heart* at a time when she was very supportive to me as my husband was ill in hospital.

Our working relationship and friendship developed over the nine years I worked with her on the teachings project and later as translator of the Yoga Upaniṣads on which she wrote the commentaries. She had asked me what I was going to do with the Sanskrit I had studied. "Look for something to translate, I suppose," I said. "I've got something for you to translate: the Yoga Upaniṣads, there are only twenty-one of them," she said as if the matter had been settled. The project was unique because there were no other published commentaries on the Yoga Upaniṣads, except for *Cūdāmani Upaniṣad* which she had completed in Bihar, where it was published in 2003. Years later she told me she had made a *sankalpa* just before she moved to Australia that she would find a translator here.

Together we collaborated on the *Yoga Tattwa, Yoga Darshana, Yoga Kundali, Nadabindu and Dhyanabindu Upanishads*. Wherever we were, at her home, on a bushwalk or at a beach, we would have long talks about the work we were doing together. She wanted us to work on *Shandilya Upanishad* next, so I started the translation and commentary in August 2019 and it was published on her birthday 26th June 2020. I then did the translation and commentary of *Triśikhī-Brāhmaṇopaniṣad*, which was published in December 2021.

For many years I was a teacher of yoga and meditation. Already a linguist, having graduated in French, Italian and Japanese from the Universities of Sydney and Queensland, Australia, I undertook four years of studies in Sanskrit at the Australian National University (ANU) with Dr McComas Taylor. I was invited to join the Golden Key Internation Society for outstanding academic achievement, as I was awarded High Distinctions throughout my Sanskrit studies.

Ruth Perini (Srimukti)
26th July 2023
yoga.upanishads@yahoo.com

www.ingramcontent.com/pod-product-compliance
Lightning Source LLC
Chambersburg PA
CBHW070255010526
44107CB00056B/2463
* 9 7 8 0 6 4 8 9 1 0 7 8 7 *